Editorial Project Manager
Lorin E. Klistoff, M.A.

Managing Editor
Karen Goldfluss, M.S. Ed.

Illustrator
Renée Christine Yates

Cover Artist
Tony Carrillo

Art Manager
Kevin Barnes

Art Director
CJae Froshay

Imaging
James Edward Grace

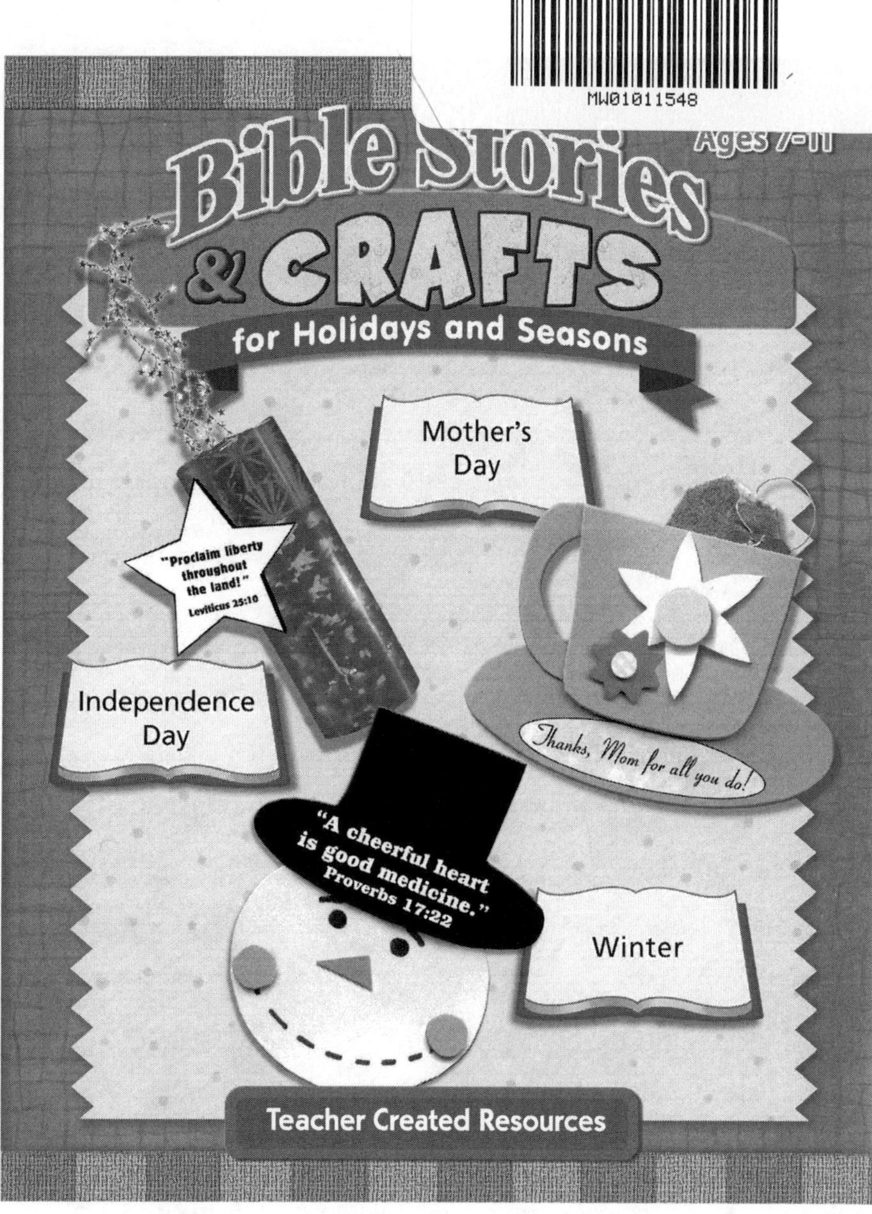

Publisher
Mary D. Smith, M.S. Ed.

Authors

Mary Tucker and Kim Rankin

Teacher Created Resources, Inc.
6421 Industry Way
Westminster, CA 92683
www.teachercreated.com

ISBN: 978-1-4206-7060-8

Reprinted, 2013
Made in U.S.A.

Table of Contents

Table of Contents

Introduction

Christian teachers are always on the lookout for creative crafts that will help them teach God's truths to children. It is relatively easy to find crafts for the holidays we celebrate throughout the year, but these projects often have no spiritual lesson or truth to accompany them. The teacher has to "wing it" and come up with his or her own Bible truth so the activity does not end up being just busy-fingers work. This book provides at least one, and usually more, creative crafts for every major holiday of the year plus some special church days, such as Ascension Day and the National Day of Prayer. Most of the holidays are secular celebrations which you may have hesitated to emphasize in the church setting before now. However, each of the holiday crafts is presented with a Bible story or lesson that will help your students think about these holidays in a new way. For example, one of the lessons for Independence Day involves an explanation of Old Testament festivals which God encouraged His people to celebrate. Children will discover that God wants us to enjoy life and include Him in all our celebrations.

Also included in this book are crafts and Bible stories for the four seasons of the year—spring, summer, fall, and winter. These crafts and stories will focus children's attention on how much God cares for them and wants to be a part of their everyday lives, with special focus on His care for this earth, kindness, sharing their faith, good manners, the fruit of the Spirit, and how they are special to God.

Each craft is accompanied by a Bible story or lesson, discussion questions, and a Bible verse you may want your students to memorize. (*Note:* This book uses the New International Version of the Bible.) Clear step-by-step directions and a list of materials needed are provided for each craft.

Many of the Bible stories are old favorites such as conquering Jericho, Hannah and Samuel, Abraham and Sarah, and Daniel and the lions. Others are less familiar such as David's advice to Solomon, Jethro and Moses, and Nicodemus' visit to Jesus. The stories are presented in a variety of ways so that even the most familiar ones will seem new and fresh to your students.

May these stories and crafts help your students look at familiar holidays and seasons with new eyes and discover how they can include the Lord in all the days they celebrate.

New Year's Day

Bible Story: King David (2 Samuel 7; 1 Kings 2:1-4)

Say this Bible story rap and have the children do the actions with you.

Israel's first king, Saul, was bad!	*(Hold up one finger.)*
He disobeyed God. It was so sad.	*(Look sad.)*
So God chose someone to take his place—	*(Point toward heaven.)*
A shepherd boy with a happy face.	*(Smile big.)*
He didn't look like a king, but God knew best	*(Shake head no, then point toward heaven.)*
'Cause David had a heart that could stand the test.	*(Put hand over heart.)*
He became the greatest king Israel ever knew	*(Spread arms out.)*
And followed God in everything he'd do.	*(Point toward heaven.)*
"Your kingdom will last forevermore,"	*(Place fist on open hand.)*
Was the message to David from the Lord.	*(Point toward heaven.)*
David prayed, "There's no one like You,	*(Fold hands and look toward heaven.)*
How great You are Lord, always true."	*(Raise hands toward heaven.)*
Throughout David's life he trusted God's plans.	*(Point toward heaven.)*
He wrote, "My times are in Your hands."	*(Pretend to write.)*
For forty years David reigned as king,	*("Flash" ten fingers four times.)*
And God blessed him in everything.	*(Hold up one finger.)*
David never worried; he was in God's care,	*(Shake head no and point toward heaven.)*
Everyday and everywhere.	*(Hold out one hand, then the other.)*

Discussion

How do you think David's trust in God helped him through all the changes in his life over the years? Will trusting God keep us from trouble and pain? How does trusting God help us in hard times? We can look forward to every new day when, like David, our "times" are in God's hands. What would you like God to do in your life this year?

Memory Verse

"This is the day the Lord has made; let us rejoice and be glad in it." (Psalm 118:24)

Even "bad" days are good when we are in God's hands. How can we be sure we are in His hands every day of every year?

New Year's Day

Craft: Time Capsule

Materials

- patterns on pages 6 and 7
- crayons or markers
- chip can or tennis ball can
- white paper
- tape or glue
- scissors

Directions

1. Copy the patterns on pages 6 and 7 on white paper.
2. Color the pattern from page 7 and wrap it lengthwise around a chip or tennis ball can.
3. Tape or glue it on.
4. Fill out the "All About Me" sheet and cut it out. Place it in your time capsule.
5. Place special items from this year in the time capsule (a family photo, movie or ballgame ticket, a lock of your hair, your favorite newspaper cartoon, a coin with this year's date on it, a school paper with a good grade, etc.).
6. Put the time capsule in a good hiding place. Plan to open it in two or three years.

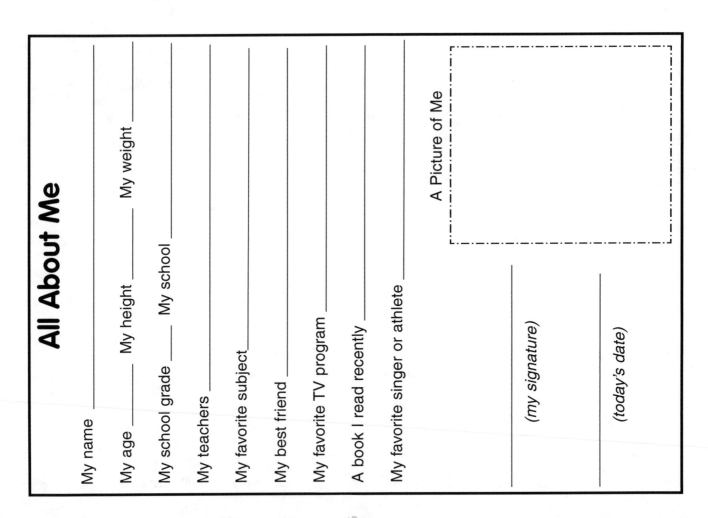

All About Me

My name ______________________

My age ______ My height ______ My weight ______

My school grade ______ My school ______________

My teachers ______________________

My favorite subject ______________________

My best friend ______________________

My favorite TV program ______________________

A book I read recently ______________________

My favorite singer or athlete ______________________

A Picture of Me

____
(my signature)

____
(today's date)

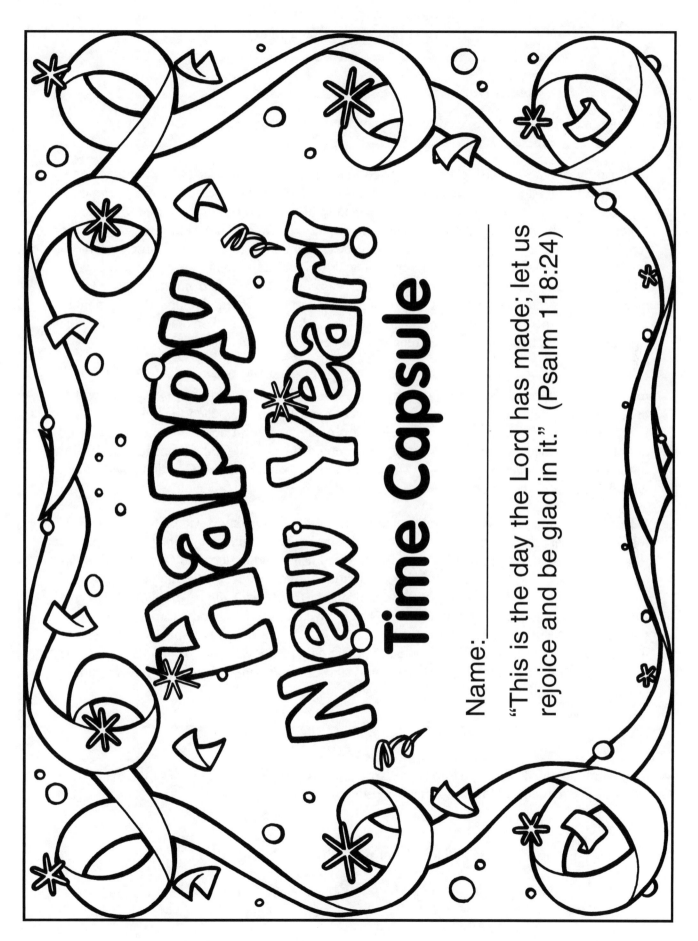

Happy New Year!

Time Capsule

Name:___________________________

"This is the day the Lord has made; let us rejoice and be glad in it." (Psalm 118:24)

New Year's Day

Bible Story: Ezra Reads God's Word (Nehemiah 8)

Have children do simple actions, as directed, to make this story come alive. Tell the story as follows:

For many years most Jewish people had lived in the Persian Empire, far from their homeland. Judah and Israel had been conquered by their enemies and most of the people had been taken captive. Many years later, a new king was in charge of Persia, one who was kind to the Jews. When the king's Jewish cup-bearer, Nehemiah, requested permission to return to Jerusalem to rebuild the walls around the city, the king agreed. Nehemiah encouraged and organized the Jewish people who had returned to Jerusalem, and they started working on the broken-down wall. (*Pretend to hammer and stack stones.*) It was not easy. People from nearby countries harassed the workers and even threatened them, trying to make them give up. But Nehemiah encouraged the people by reminding them that the Lord would help them succeed. In less than two months, the Jerusalem wall was repaired. (*Raise hands in victory.*)

Nehemiah arranged a great celebration when the work was done. The people gathered in the town square to listen to Ezra, the priest, read the *Book of the Law*, God's Word. Ezra stood on a high platform so all the people could see and hear him. When he opened the holy book, all the people stood up. (*Stand up.*) Ezra read aloud from daybreak until noon, and the people stood quietly and listened attentively. Many of them wept as they heard God's Word for the first time in their lives. (*Put hands over face.*) Then Ezra and the people praised God and bowed down with their faces to the ground to worship Him. (*Bow down.*)

When the reading was over, Nehemiah said to the people, "This day is sacred to the Lord." He told them to eat and drink and enjoy themselves, sharing with their neighbors. The people went away and celebrated with great joy because they had heard and understood God's Word. (*Jump and raise hands in the air with joy.*) The celebration lasted for seven days, and each day began with Ezra reading the *Book of the Law* to the people. (*Hold hands out as if holding an open Bible.*) The people did not get tired of it. They were eager to know God's Law. All the years they had been captives in other lands, they had not heard it; now it was a special treat. Though it made them sad to discover that they had unknowingly disobeyed many of God's laws, they were happy to finally know them so they could start obeying Him. They knew how important God's Word was to their everyday lives.

Discussion

Why do you think the people stood up when Ezra began reading the *Book of the Law*? What does God's Word mean to you? How has it made a difference in your life?

Bible Verse

"Your word is a lamp to my feet and a light for my path." (Psalm 119:105)

How can God's Word light your way through every day of the year?

Craft: Bible Verse Chain

Materials

- patterns on pages 9 and 10
- white paper
- pen and markers
- tape or glue
- scissors

Directions

1. Copy patterns on white paper.
2. Write Bible verses for the New Year on the paper strips.
3. Cut the strips apart. Color the Happy New Year strip.
4. Loop the first strip into a circle and tape or glue the ends together.
5. Loop the next strip into a circle, linking it with the first one before you tape or glue the ends. Continue linking all the strips together to form a paper chain.

Finished Product

"Your word is a lamp to my feet and a light for my path." (Psalm 119:105)

Teach me knowledge and good judgment, for I believe in your commands." (Psalm 119:66)

New Year's Day

Teach us to number our days aright, that we may gain a heart of wisdom. (Psalm 90:12)

Valentine's Day

Bible Story: The Rich Young Man (Matthew 19:16-26)

Choose a student to act the part of the rich young man, with you playing the part of Jesus. You will also need a narrator.

Narrator:	One day a young man came up to Jesus to ask Him a question.
Young Man:	Teacher, what good thing must I do to get eternal life?
Jesus:	Obey the commandments.
Young Man:	Which ones?
Narrator:	Jesus quickly summarized the commandments.
Young Man:	I have kept them all.
Narrator:	Jesus knew all about him and knew what was holding him back.
Jesus:	Sell all your possessions and give the money to the poor. If you do this, you will have treasure in heaven. Then come and follow me.
Narrator:	The young man was rich and trusted more in his riches than in God. He didn't want to give up what he had, so he went away sad. His response made Jesus sad, too.
Jesus:	It is very hard for a rich person to enter the kingdom of heaven.
Narrator:	A person with many possessions or a lot of money often loves that money more than he or she loves God. Jesus understood that the rich young man couldn't bring himself to choose between his possessions and God. Then Jesus said to His disciples:
Jesus:	"With man this is impossible, but with God all things are possible."
Narrator:	When a person truly wants to follow Jesus, God will give him or her the strength to leave other things behind. The rich young man's heart was set on his riches rather than on pleasing God. He gave up forgiveness for his sins and a home in heaven for money that would not last. How sad!

Discussion

What kept the rich young man from following Jesus? How can "things" keep us from God?

Bible Verse

"Since, then, you have been raised with Christ, set your hearts on things above, where Christ is seated at the right hand of God." (Colossians 3:1)

What does it mean to "set your heart" on something? Is your heart set on God?

Valentine's Day

Craft: Tissue Paper Valentine

Finished Product

Materials

- pattern below
- red and white tissue paper
- glue
- white cardstock
- heart pattern
- scissors

Directions

1. Copy the pattern on white cardstock and cut out the heart.
2. Cut one-inch squares of red and white tissue paper.
3. Apply glue to the heart in small dots forming a pattern. Twist tissue paper squares and place them on the glue dots.
4. Give it to your special valentine.

Variation: Use glitter or sequins instead of tissue paper.

". . . set your hearts on things above, where
Christ is seated at the right hand of God."
(Colossians 3:1)

Valentine's Day

Bible Story: David and Jonathan (1 Samuel 18:1-4; 20:1-42; 23:15-18)

Let each student choose a partner to pantomime this story as you tell it. One will be David and the other will be Jonathan. Encourage them to listen closely to the story; then act it out together. Some suggestions are provided in the story.

David and Jonathan first met when David fought and defeated Goliath the giant. (*Have partners shake hands or hug each other.*) King Saul was impressed with the young shepherd boy's courage and strength, and he invited David to live with him and his son Jonathan. The Bible says that Jonathan became one in spirit with David and that he loved him as himself. Though Jonathan was a king's son and David was just a shepherd, they became best friends. As a sign of friendship, Jonathan took off the robe he was wearing and gave it to David. He also gave David his sword and his bow and arrows. (*Partners may act this out.*) Jonathan was a generous friend.

Jonathan was also a loyal friend. His father, Saul, grew jealous of David and wanted to kill him. Jonathan tried to talk his father out of it, but when Saul angrily threw a spear at his own son, Jonathan knew it was useless. He was so sad, he couldn't eat. And he was deeply ashamed for his father's shameful treatment of David.

The next morning, Jonathan went out into a field to shoot his bow and arrows. He took a boy with him to run after the arrows and bring them back after he shot them. Jonathan and David had planned for David to hide in the field. If Jonathan shot an arrow and told the boy, "The arrow is beyond you. Run quickly to find it," David would know that Saul was after him and he needed to run away. Jonathan shot an arrow (*One partner can pretend to shoot a bow and arrow; the other should hide.*) beyond the boy and said to him exactly what he had promised David he would say. Then Jonathan sent the boy home. David came out from his hiding place to say goodbye to his best friend. They both knew he had to leave because Jonathan could not protect him from Saul. The two friends were so sad, they cried together. "Go in peace," Jonathan told David, "for we have sworn friendship with each other in the name of the Lord." (*Partners may hug each other or say goodbye in another way; then one leaves and the other waves goodbye.*) David went away and Jonathan went home.

The two friends saw each other only once more. When Saul was chasing David to kill him in the Desert of Ziph, Jonathan came for a brief meeting with David to encourage him. (*One partner may pat the other on the back with encouragement.*) "Don't be afraid," Jonathan said. "My father Saul will not lay a hand on you. You will be king over Israel." As the king's son, Jonathan would have been next in line to be king, but he realized that God had chosen David for that honor, and it was all right with him.

Discussion

How did Jonathan show his love for David? How can you show your love for your friends?

Bible Verse

"Dear friends, let us love one another, for love comes from God." (1 John 4:7a)

When we love God, He helps us love other people as Jonathan loved David.

Valentine's Day

Craft: Candy Cane Heart Card

Materials

- white cardstock
- two wrapped candy canes
- pattern below
- glue
- scissors

Directions

1. Copy the heart pattern on white cardstock.
2. Cut the heart out and glue two candy canes on it to form a heart.
3. Give the card to your special valentine.

Variation: Use red and white pipe cleaners twisted together to form a candy cane. Glue them on the heart.

"Dear friends,
let us love one another,
for love comes from God."
(1 John 4:7a)

Palm Sunday

Bible Story: Jesus Enters Jerusalem (Matthew 21:1-11; Mark 11:1-11)

Have students line up along an imaginary road which you walk along as you tell the story. Let them pretend to be the welcoming crowd, laying their coats in the road, waving their hands, and quietly praising Jesus as you go by. They can praise Jesus more enthusiastically and less quietly later after they make paper palm branches and repeat the praise poem.

Jesus and His disciples were close to Jerusalem when he sent two of them to a nearby village. He told them they would find a donkey and her colt tied up. They were to untie them and bring them back to Jesus. If someone tried to stop them, the disciples were to say, "The Lord needs them." The two disciples did what Jesus had told them. When they got back, they placed their outer robes on the donkey and the colt and Jesus sat on them and began riding them into the city of Jerusalem.

A large crowd of people gathered along the road to see Jesus. Some had heard about the miracles He performed and were eager to see Him for themselves. Others had actually seen Him heal the sick and give sight to the blind and even raise the dead. Some of them had probably been in the crowd of five thousand He had miraculously fed with five small loaves of bread and two fish. They had wanted to make Him their king after that experience, but He would not allow it. Now they were welcoming Jesus to Jerusalem like a king. They were so excited to see Him, many of them threw their robes down on the road for Him to ride over. Others picked branches from palm trees and threw them down on the road. Many followed behind Jesus, making a parade through the town. They shouted, "Hosanna to the Son of David! Blessed is he who comes in the name of the Lord."

The whole city was stirred up by all the noise and commotion. Jesus rode into town quietly on a donkey, but He was greeted like a great king or a conquering hero, like a military leader who has defeated the enemy. Jesus had not been in Jerusalem often, so the people who lived there did not recognize Him. Many asked who He was. "This is Jesus, the prophet from Nazareth in Galilee," some people said. These were probably people from Galilee who were visiting the city. Jesus had taught and performed miracles throughout Galilee, so they recognized Him as a great man, but not as the Son of God. Most did not understand His true identity, but they were glad to see Him and welcomed Him warmly.

Discussion

Why did people welcome Jesus so enthusiastically to Jerusalem? What are some ways we can praise Him today?

Bible Verse

"Let the name of the Lord be praised, both now and forevermore." (Psalm 113:2)

How do you like to praise the Lord?

Palm Sunday

Craft: Palm Branch

Materials

- patterns on page 17
- wooden paint stirrer
- black fine-tip marker
- green cardstock
- glue or stapler
- scissors

Directions

1. Cut out the patterns and trace them on green cardstock. You will need two large, six medium, and five small.
2. Cut out the leaves. Glue or staple them to a paint stirrer with the smallest leaves at the top as shown, getting larger as you go down to form a palm branch.
3. Print Psalm 113:2 on the paint stirrer: "Let the name of the Lord be praised, both now and forevermore."

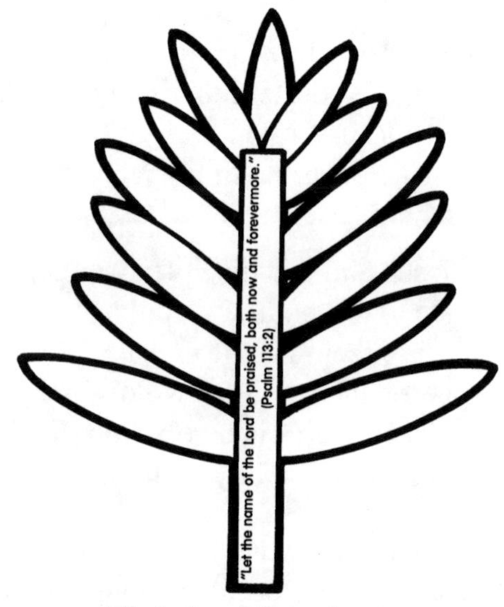

Finished Product

Praise Poem

(say while waving palm branch)

"Hosanna! Hosanna!
Welcome David's Son,
Coming in the Lord's name;
Praise Him everyone!
Hosanna! Hosanna!
Wave your palm branch high.
Thank the Lord above
As Jesus Christ comes by."

Craft: Palm Branch *(cont.)*

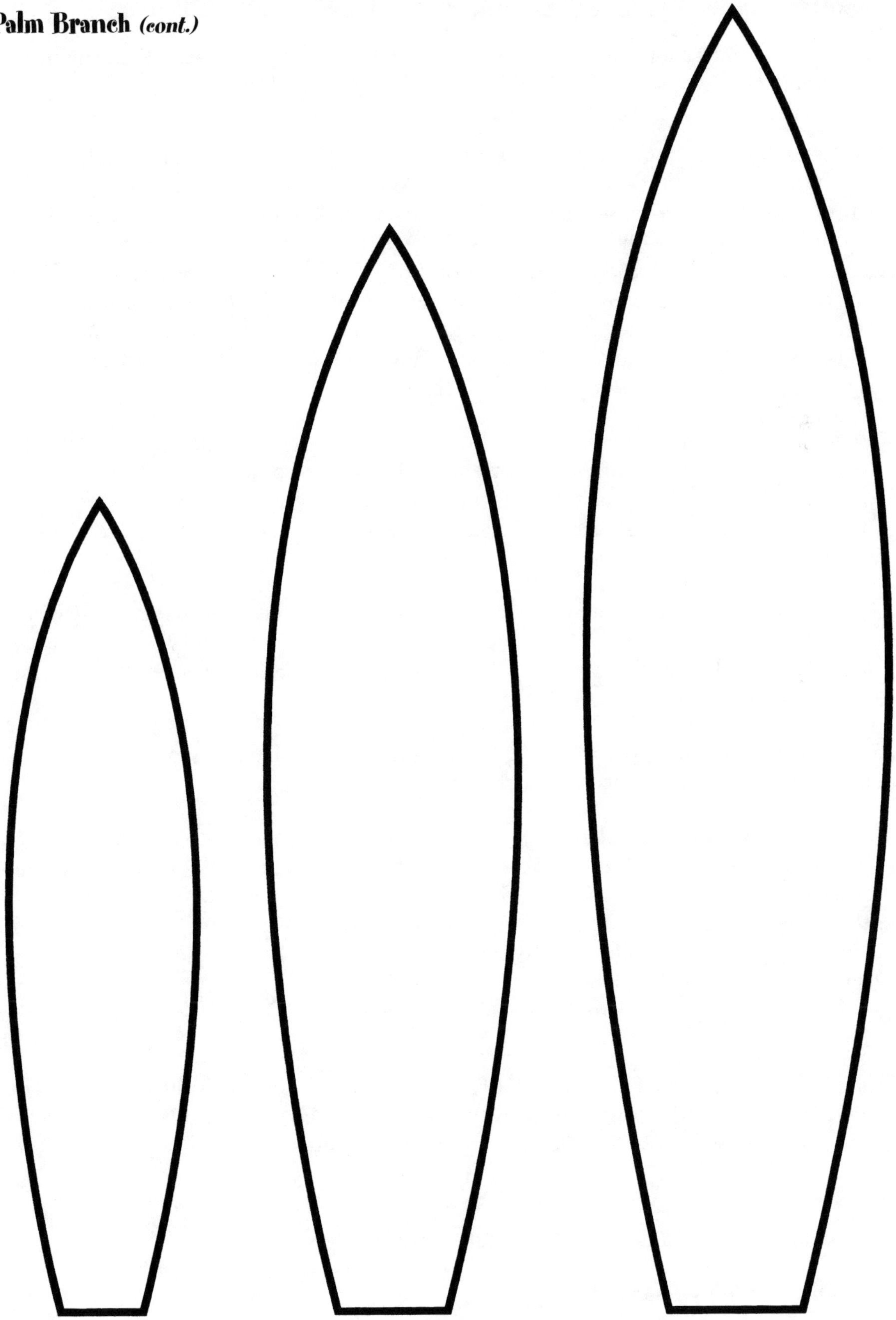

Palm Sunday

Bible Story: Fulfilled Prophecy (Matthew 21:1-11; Luke 19:28-42)

Tell students that you want them to listen carefully to what you say, and every time you mention *prophecy* or the *Old Testament,* they should hold their hands out like an open Bible.

The first Palm Sunday was a joyous, exciting occasion with the people of Jerusalem throwing their robes on the road for Jesus' donkey to step on, waving palm branches, and shouting praises to God as He rode into town. It was also an event that had been planned for hundreds of years. Zechariah, an Old Testament prophet who lived hundreds of years before Jesus was born, wrote: "Rejoice greatly, O Daughter of Zion! Shout, Daughter of Jerusalem! See, your king comes to you, righteous and having salvation, gentle and riding on a donkey, on a colt, the foal of a donkey." (Zechariah 9:9) (*Students should hold out "open Bible" hands.*) How did he know what was going to happen? God revealed it to him because God already had a plan for Jesus' Triumphal Entry into Jerusalem.

Why did God plan for Jesus to ride into town on a donkey? Kings and important people usually rode magnificent horses. A donkey was a symbol of peace, and Jesus came to be the Prince of Peace as Isaiah prophesied He would be: "And he will be called Wonderful Counselor, Mighty God, Everlasting Father, Prince of Peace." (Isaiah 9:6) (*Students should hold out "open Bible" hands.*)

As the people welcomed Him to the city, many of them shouted, "Blessed is He who comes in the name of the Lord!" Those words are from Psalm 118:26 in the Old Testament. (*Students should hold out "open Bible" hands.*) The book of Psalms has many verses that talk about Jesus, written centuries before He came.

Some religious leaders did not like the way people were praising Jesus as He came into the city. They said to Him, "Teacher, rebuke your disciples!"

Jesus answered by quoting Habakkuk, another Old Testament prophet. (*Students should hold out "open Bible" hands.*) "If they keep quiet, the stones will cry out," He said. (a paraphrase of Habakkuk 2:11). Jesus was God's Son and deserved to be praised. Sadly, many of the people who shouted praises to Him as He rode into Jerusalem on Palm Sunday changed their minds about Him and shouted for His death later that week. But Jesus already knew everything that would happen.

Discussion

Why is it important for us to know how Old Testament prophecies were fulfilled at Jesus' Triumphal Entry into Jerusalem? If Jesus already knew that the people who welcomed Him on Sunday would call for His death on Friday, why didn't He just stay away from Jerusalem?

Bible Verse

". . . Blessed is he who comes in the name of the Lord!" (Mark 11:9)

Why do you think Jesus deserves to be praised?

Palm Sunday

Craft: Palm Sunday Picture

Materials

- patterns on pages 19 and 20
- white cardstock
- craft stick
- glue or tape
- crayons or markers
- scissors

Finished Product

Directions

1. Copy the patterns on white cardstock and color them.
2. Cut a slit in the town scene.
3. Cut out Jesus and the donkey. Glue or tape a craft stick to the back of the figure.
4. Slide the stick through the slit on the town scene. Move it slowly from the left to the right to show Jesus riding into town.

“. . . Blessed is he who comes in the name of the Lord!”
(Mark 11:9)

Good Friday

Bible Story: Jesus Dies (Luke 23:26-43; John 19:17-30)

As you tell the story of Jesus' crucifixion, follow the directions for sketching simple symbols on the board to help children understand and remember what happened.

Many people loved Jesus and believed what He said, but some religious leaders were jealous of the attention He got. They hated Him so much they planned to kill Him. They carried out their plan to have Jesus arrested, then tried Him in a mock trial that broke all the rules. When the Roman governor, Pilate, would have released Him, Jesus' enemies screamed for His death, and Pilate finally gave in.

Soldiers forced Jesus to carry His own cross to a hill called Golgotha outside the city. Jesus was so weak from being badly beaten by the soldiers, He fell and did not have the strength to carry the cross anymore. The soldiers forced a man named Simon, who was watching, to carry the cross the rest of the way to the hill. (*Draw a hill on the board.*) The soldiers nailed Jesus' hands and feet to the cross and raised the cross. (*Draw a cross on the hill.*) Two convicted thieves were hung on crosses to die next to Him. (*Draw a cross on each side of the center cross.*) One of the thieves insulted Jesus and said to Him, "Save yourself and us!"

The other one said to his fellow thief, "Don't you fear God? We deserve this punishment, but this man has done nothing wrong." Then he said to Jesus, "Jesus, remember me when you come into your kingdom," showing that he believed in Jesus.

Jesus told the thief, "Today you will be with me in paradise."

Pilate had someone make a sign and attach it to Jesus' cross. It said "Jesus of Nazareth, the King of the Jews." (*Draw this sign on the center cross.*) Some religious leaders tried to get Pilate to remove the sign because they said it was not true, but he refused. Some of Jesus' closest friends and family, including His mother, stood near His cross for hours to be with Him as His life ended. (*Draw stick figures beneath the center cross.*)

After many hours of suffering terrible pain hanging on the cross, Jesus said, "It is finished." Then He died. But it was not the Roman soldiers or the Jewish religious leaders who put Jesus to death. It was our sins that put Him on the cross. (*Write "OUR SINS" on the center cross.*) He willingly died to take the punishment for our sins. That is why we call the day of Jesus' death *Good* Friday.

Good Friday

Bible Story: Jesus Dies (Luke 23:26-43; John 19:17-30) *(cont.)*

Discussion

Jesus died for people's sins. Does that mean everyone's sins have been forgiven? Why or why not? Why do you think Jesus was willing to die for your sins? How can we show Jesus we are thankful that He died for us?

Bible Verse

"But God demonstrates his own love for us in this: While we were still sinners, Christ died for us." (Romans 5:8)

The cross is a symbol that reminds us of two very important things—our sins and Jesus' love. He "demonstrated" or proved His love by dying for us.

Craft: Stained Glass Paper Cross

Materials

- pattern on page 23
- white cardstock
- black construction paper
- tissue paper (various colors)
- waxed paper
- scissors
- glue

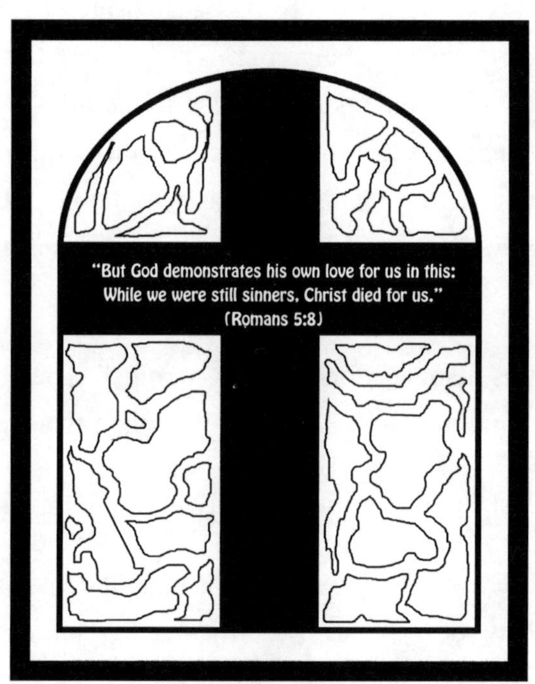

Finished Product

Directions

1. Copy the pattern on white cardstock.
2. Cut around the cross as indicated.
3. Between two sheets of waxed paper, place small colored pieces of tissue paper.
4. Glue together the two sheets of waxed paper.
5. Glue the waxed paper to the back of the cross.
6. Mount the project on black paper for a frame.

Variation: Melt crayon shavings between the sheets of waxed paper.

Good Friday

cut out

cut out

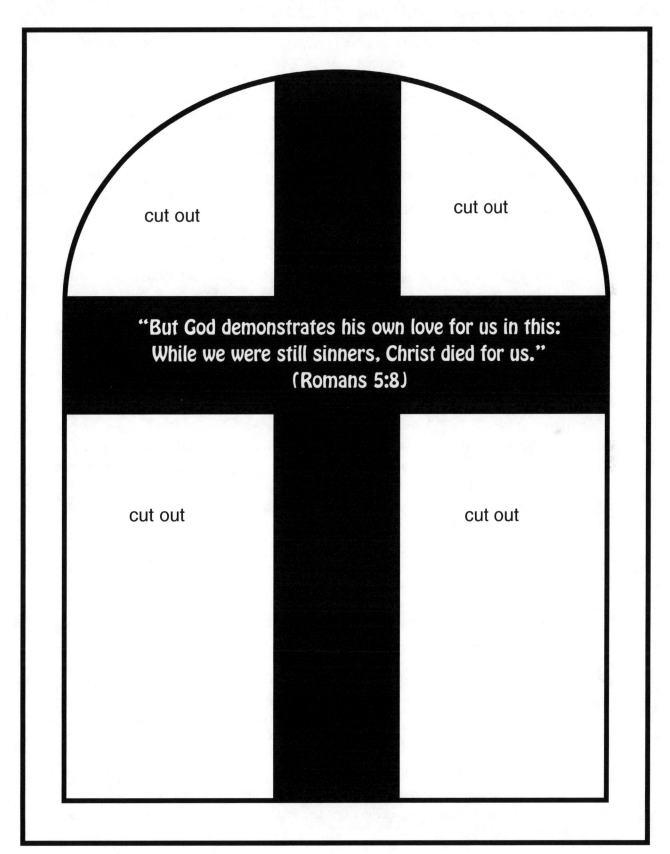

"But God demonstrates his own love for us in this:
While we were still sinners, Christ died for us."
(Romans 5:8)

cut out

cut out

Good Friday

Bible Story: A Day to Remember (Matthew 27:22-31, 45-60)

Read the story below as a news reporter telling about what is happening. You will need a couple of students to read the parts of the teacher and the priest.

Reporter: I am standing on Mount Calvary where Jesus, the miracle worker, was crucified today. It is over now, but it is something I will never forget. It began about nine o'clock this morning when the soldiers brought Jesus up here on the hill. They nailed Him to the cross. Jesus asked God to forgive them, saying they did not know what they were doing. Everyone heard Him. He hung there all day, seeming barely alive. He was offered some wine to ease His pain, but Jesus refused it. At about noon everything became as dark as night and stayed dark until about three o'clock. When He died, some frightening things happened. Here to tell us about one of these things is a priest who was in the temple earlier today. Can you tell us what happened?

Priest: I was standing in the temple when the great curtain that separates the holy place from the holy of holies suddenly started ripping in half, from the top to the bottom. It was almost as if a huge hand took hold of it and just tore it, but no one was there. I can't explain it! It was frightening! Everyone could see into the holy of holies, which is a thing that is never allowed!

Reporter: It seems that this ripping of the temple curtain occurred at the exact moment that Jesus died. Right after that happened, a powerful earthquake shook the ground. It knocked me down and scared me half to death! We have reports that the earthquake opened up some tombs around Jerusalem. Isn't that right, sir? Did you see this happen?

Teacher: Yes, I was walking by an area where there are several tombs when the earthquake hit. I hung onto a tree as I watched the stones of some of the tombs roll away. Then some of the dead actually came out of their tombs and started walking around. I do not know where they went or what happened next because I ran away from there as fast as I could!

Reporter: We have reports that some of them were seen in Jerusalem. Such a thing has never happened before. We cannot explain it or the other events. They seem to all be related to Jesus' death. One of the soldiers standing near me by Jesus' cross was so shaken by the earthquake, I heard him say, "Surely, he was the Son of God."

Jesus' body was taken down from the cross a little while ago by Joseph, a rich man from Arimathea. He buried Jesus in his own tomb. The stone has been rolled across the door and that seems to be the end of all the unusual events for now.

Good Friday

Bible Story: A Day to Remember (Matthew 27:22-31, 45-60) *(cont.)*

Discussion

What unusual things happened on the day Jesus died? Why do you think God made these things happen? What even more unusual event took place three days later?

Bible Verse

"He was delivered over to death for our sins and was raised to life for our justification." (Romans 4:25)

Who "delivered" Jesus over to death? His enemies thought they were in charge of His death, but they were actually carrying out God's plan of salvation!

Craft: Glitter/Bead Cross

Materials

- pattern on page 26
- glitter or sequins
- colored markers
- white cardstock
- glue

Directions

1. Copy page 26 on white cardstock and color it.
2. Cover the cross with glue.
3. Sprinkle glitter or sequins on the glue.
4. Shake off excess glitter or sequins over a waste basket.

Finished Product

Variation

Cover the cross with beads by following these directions.

1. You will need the following materials: one heart-shaped pony bead, 25 (12mm) faceted crystal beads, and two white pipe cleaners.
2. Cut the pipe cleaners into these sizes: three 2 1/2", one 1", and one 5 1/2".
3. Place the heart-shaped pony bead in the middle of the one-inch pipe cleaner. Poke the pipe cleaner in the two holes of the heart. Fold the ends of the pipe cleaner at the back to secure them.
4. String two 2 1/2" pipe cleaners with four beads and the other with five beads.
5. Poke the five-beaded pipe cleaner in the two holes at the top of the cross. Poke the four-beaded pipe cleaners in the holes on the cross bar.
6. String 16 beads on the 5 1/2" pipe cleaner. Poke it in the holes going down the length of the cross.
7. Tape the ends of the bent pipe cleaners down on the back to secure them.

Good Friday

"He was delivered over to death for our sins and was raised to life for our justification." (Romans 4:25)

Easter

Bible Story: Jesus Is Alive! (Luke 24:1-12)

Teach children this song and have them sing it with you to review Jesus' resurrection day.

(*Tune:* "I Will Make You Fishers of Men")

1

Early in the morning one day,
Some women went along the way.
They were headed for Jesus' tomb,
But He wasn't there.
Gave them quite a scare
When He wasn't there.
Angels clothed in gleaming white robes
Said He wasn't there.

2

"He has risen, just as He said.
He is alive, no longer dead."
All the women bowed to the ground
For He wasn't there.
Gave them quite a scare
When He wasn't there.
Told disciples what they had seen.
Jesus wasn't there.

3

His disciples did not believe
He was alive. They only grieved.
Peter ran and looked in the tomb,
But He wasn't there.
Jesus wasn't there.
Gave them quite a scare
They all found it hard to believe
That He wasn't there.

Discussion

Why do you think the women went to Jesus' tomb? (Read Mark 16:1.) Why didn't they get to do what they planned? Why do you think Jesus' disciples didn't believe Jesus had risen?

Bible Verse

"We have peace with God through our Lord Jesus Christ." (Romans 5:1)

What is the only way to have peace with God?

Easter

Craft: 3-D Easter Card

Materials

- patterns on pages 28–30
- white paper
- crayons or markers
- white cardstock
- tape
- scissors

Directions

1. Copy the lily pattern on page 29 on white cardstock. Flip the paper over and copy the cross pattern, page 30, on the inside of the card.
2. Fold the card in half. Color the inside of the cross and the flowers.
3. Copy the "He Is Risen" pattern on white paper (not cardstock). Cut it out. Fold on the dashed lines. Tape the flaps to the inside top of the card. Tape one flap to each side as shown.

Finished Product

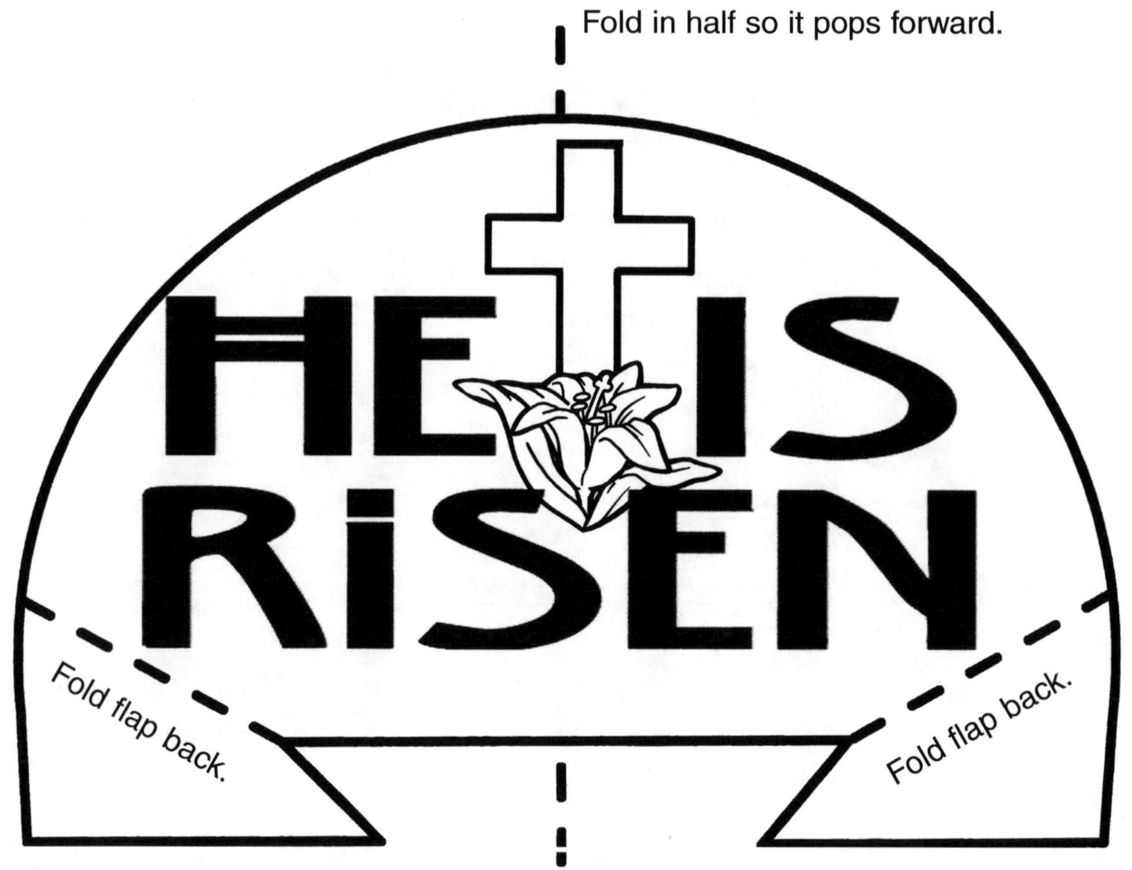

Jesus died but came to life again,
so you could have forgiveness for sin!

"We have peace with God
through our Lord Jesus Christ."
(Romans 5:1)

Easter

Bible Story: An Empty Tomb (Matthew 27:62–28:15)

As you tell the Bible story, ask students questions to guide their thinking and focus their attention.

After Jesus had died and was buried, the chief priests and some Pharisees went to Governor Pilate and told him, "While He was still alive, the deceiver said He would rise again after three days. We want to make sure His disciples do not steal His body and tell everyone that He rose from the dead."

Why do you think they called Jesus the "deceiver"? Was Jesus ever dishonest? What do you think they asked Pilate to do? They asked Pilate to place soldiers at Jesus' tomb to guard it. Pilate did what they asked, and he even put a seal on the stone that covered the door of the tomb to make sure no one tried to open it.

On the Sunday after Jesus' death, some women went to Jesus' tomb. *What did they see?* The women saw an angel sitting on the stone that had been rolled away from the door of the tomb. *How did the guards respond to the angel?* They shook with fear. *What did the angel tell the women?* The angel told the women that Jesus was not in the tomb; He had risen from the dead! "Go quickly and tell His disciples that He has risen and they will see Him in Galilee," he said.

While the women were hurrying off to tell the disciples, who do you think they saw? They saw Jesus. He told them not to be afraid. In the meantime, the soldiers who had been guarding the tomb went to report to the chief priests what had happened. *How do you think the chief priests felt about what the guards had to tell them?* The chief priests met with the elders and came up with a plan. They agreed to pay the guards to lie about what had happened. The guards were told to say that they had fallen asleep and that Jesus' disciples had come and stolen His body during the night. The guards agreed and that's the story they told. *What was wrong with their story; why didn't it sound reasonable?* Of course, a Roman soldier would have been instantly executed if he had ever fallen asleep on duty and allowed such a thing to happen. But some people believed their story. Those who followed Jesus, though, knew exactly why the tomb was empty—He was alive!

Discussion

What happened to the guards Jesus' enemies were depending on to guard His tomb? Why do you think the chief priest and elders paid the guards to lie about what had happened?

Bible Verse

"For no matter how many promises God has made, they are 'Yes' in Christ." (2 Corinthians 1:20a)

How do you know Jesus' death and resurrection were all part of God's great promises?

Easter

Craft: Bible Promise Egg

Materials

- patterns on pages 33–36
- white paper
- hole punch
- glue
- white cardstock
- crayons or markers
- yarn
- scissors

Finished Product

Directions

1. On white cardstock, copy the egg pattern on page 33 twice. Copy this page on white paper.
2. Color and cut out the art below. Glue it on the egg. Add your own decorations.
3. Holding the two patterns on top of each other, use a hole punch to punch holes most of the way around the egg.
4. Tie a knot in one end of the yarn and weave it in and out to sew the egg together, making a pocket. Leave the top open.
5. Copy and cut apart the Bible verse strips on pages 34–36. Store them in the egg pocket. Take them out to memorize God's promises.

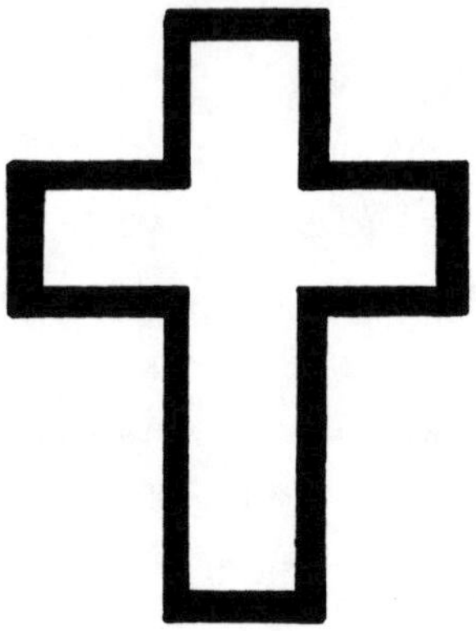

"For no matter how many promises God has made, they are 'Yes' in Christ."

(2 Corinthians 1:20a)

Easter

"If you remain in me and my words remain in you, ask whatever you wish, and it will be given you."

(John 15:7)

". . . In this world you will have trouble. But take heart! I have overcome the world."

(John 16:33)

"Blessed are the pure in heart, for they will see God."

(Matthew 5:8)

"But seek first his kingdom and his righteousness, and all these things will be given to you as well."

(Matthew 6:33)

"For the Lord is good and his love endures forever . . . ."

(Psalm 100:5)

Easter

"Peace I leave with you; my peace I give you."

(John 14:27)

"Cast all your anxiety on him because he cares for you."

(1 Peter 5:7)

"If we confess our sins, he is faithful and just and will forgive us our sins and purify us from all unrighteousness."

(1 John 1:9)

"I can do everything through him who gives me strength."

(Philippians 4:13)

". . . I have loved you with an everlasting love; I have drawn you with loving-kindness."

(Jeremiah 31:3)

Easter

"Put on the full armor of God so that you can take your stand against the devil's schemes."

(Ephesians 6:11)

"Look, he is coming with the clouds, and every eye will see him . . . ."

(Revelation 1:7)

"The prayer of a righteous man is powerful and effective."

(James 5:16b)

"And my God will meet all your needs according to his glorious riches in Christ Jesus."

(Philippians 4:19)

"For God so loved the world that he gave his one and only Son, that whoever believes in him shall not perish but have eternal life."

(John 3:16)

Easter

Craft: Open-and-Close Tomb Scene

Materials

- patterns on pages 37 and 38
- white paper
- crayons
- tape
- scissors

Directions

1. Copy the patterns on white paper and color the scene and the rock.
2. Cut out the rock and tape it on one side over the tomb door.
3. Flip over the rock to see the message of Easter.

"... he has risen, just as he said."
(Matthew 28:6a)

Finished Product

Rock Pattern

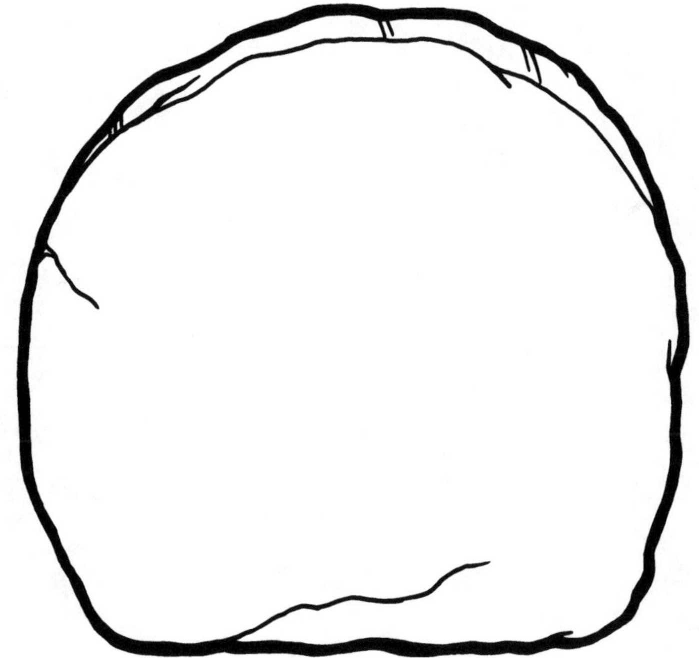

“. . . he has risen, just as he said.”
(Matthew 28:6a)
HE IS
RISEN

Easter

Bible Story: Peter Tells About Jesus' Resurrection (Acts 2:14-41)

Say this Bible story rap for students; then teach them to say it with you. Have them help you keep the rhythm with finger snapping.

Just before Jesus left His friends, He promised the Holy Spirit to them.

On Pentecost, a Jewish feast day, the Holy Spirit came in a special way.

A large crowd of people gathered around, to find out what was going down.

Peter stood up and started to preach; he had something important he wanted to teach.

He said God's the One who sent Jesus to Earth, but most people never recognized His worth.

"God handed Him over to you," Peter said, "and you nailed him to a cross until He was dead!

But God allowed Him to experience death's agony, so we could be forgiven—you and me.

Even David knew about the Lord, and wrote about Him in God's Word."

The people who believed Peter's words were true said, "Brother, what shall we do?"

"Repent," said Peter, "and be baptized! That's the way to have new life."

"Save yourselves," was Peter's last word, and many people gave their lives to the Lord.

The church grew by three thousand that day, as people began to follow Jesus' way.

Discussion

Why do you think Peter chose the topic of Jesus' resurrection for his sermon? What did Peter tell people they needed to do to have their sins forgiven? Why is Jesus' resurrection important to you?

Bible Verse

"For what I received I passed on to you as of first importance: that Christ died for our sins according to the Scriptures, that he was buried, that he was raised on the third day according to the Scriptures."
(1 Corinthians 15:3–4)

You could call this the Gospel in a nutshell because these two verses summarize the four Gospels and tell what Jesus did for us. Is knowing these verses enough to assure us of a home in heaven? Explain.

Easter

Craft: Salvation Bracelet

Materials

- one pony bead of each color (yellow, black, red, white, purple, blue, green, brown, or tan) per student
- 12 clear pony beads per student
- stretch bead cord
- scissors

Directions

1. Cut about a 10" to 12" piece of stretch cord.
2. String the beads on the cord, placing a clear pony bead between each colored bead.
3. Tie the string in a knot and trim the ends of the cord.

Meaning of Colors

1. Yellow—God loves you and wants you to be His child. (1 John 4:19)
2. Black—Sin separates you from God. (Romans 3:23)
3. Red—God sent Jesus to shed His blood for your sins so you could be forgiven. (Romans 5:8)
4. White—Jesus' death takes away your sin if you believe in Him. (1 John 1:7)
5. Blue—After you receive Jesus as your Savior, you need to be baptized and confess your faith. (Hebrews 10:22)
6. Green—God wants you to grow as a Christian. (2 Peter 3:18)
7. Purple—Someday Jesus will reward His children with a crown of life. (Revelation 2:10)

Finished Product

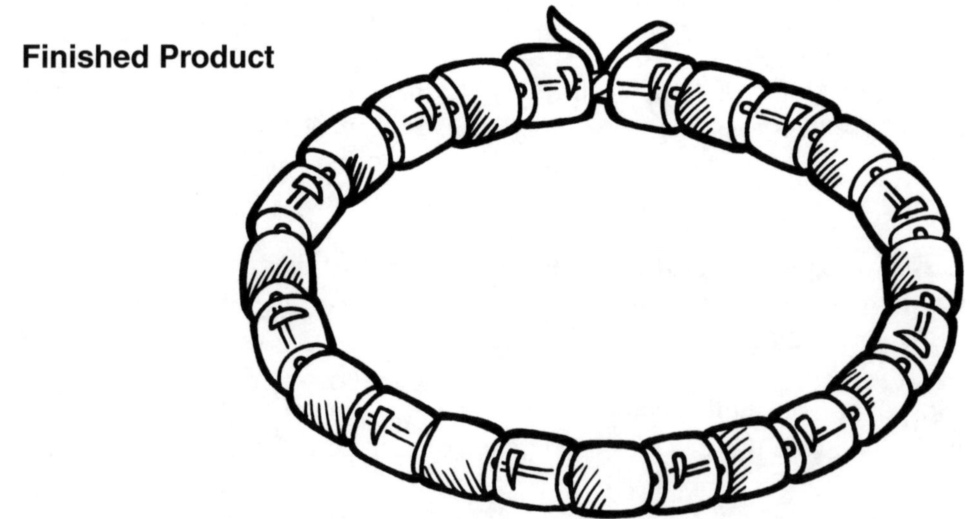

National Day of Prayer

Bible Story: Jesus Encourages Us to Pray (Matthew 6:5-13)

Print the Lord's prayer on the board or on a large sheet of poster board for everyone to see. Tell the story, then read the prayer aloud together. Ask questions, as directed below, to help students understand the prayer. Let them answer as a group.

One day Jesus was teaching about prayer. He said that prayer is a personal conversation with God. Prayer is not something to do in a loud voice on the street corner to attract attention, even though some people did that. Jesus said when people pray sincerely to God, He will answer. Some people who do not love God merely repeat the same thing over and over and call it prayer. But prayer is not a bunch of magic words that can be repeated many times to make God work. Prayer is talking to God, sharing our thoughts and feelings, telling Him we love Him, and asking Him to do His will.

Jesus gave a sample prayer that we can follow when we pray. (*Read the Lord's prayer aloud together.*)

To whom do we pray? *(Our Father in heaven)* What does it mean to say, "Hallowed be your name"? *(Holy is your name, God.)* Why do you think we tell God that we want His kingdom to come and His will to be done? *(We agree with God that we want Him to do what He knows is best.)* What do we ask God to provide? *(Our daily bread)* What does that mean? *(Provide food every day.)* What do we ask God to forgive? *(Our debts)* What does that mean? *(Our sins)* What do we say we will do? *(Forgive our debtors)* Who are our debtors? (*Those who have sinned against us*)

We ask God not to lead us into temptation. What is temptation? *(Wanting to do something wrong)* Is everyone tempted to do wrong? How often? *(Yes, all the time)* What do we want God to do for us instead? *(Deliver us from the evil one)* Who do you think is the evil one? *(Satan, the devil)*

Jesus gave us an example of how to pray, but He did not want us to always just repeat this prayer. He wants us to talk to God about everything in our own words. His sample prayer just shows us the kinds of things we should include in our prayers: praise and worship of God, requests for needs, confession of sin and a request for forgiveness, and requests for help to live for God. Jesus' sample prayer does not mention specific things; but when we pray, we should be specific. For example, instead of just asking God to forgive our sins, we should confess exactly what we have done and ask Him to forgive each specific sin. When we ask Him to provide for our needs, we should tell Him exactly what we need, or what someone else needs.

Why is prayer so important in a Christian's life? (*Let students share their ideas.*) Even Jesus, God's Son, prayed. Why do you think He prayed? (*Students' ideas may include that Jesus loved to talk to His Father and that He prayed for strength to do what He knew God wanted Him to do.*)

Jesus did not say we have to be in a certain place to pray. We do not have to be in a certain position, such as bowing down or with our eyes closed. We can pray when we are traveling in a car. There are no certain words we have to use. We can talk to God the way we talk to our parents, with respect and love. Anytime, any place, anyhow—that is how we can pray.

National Day of Prayer

Bible Story: Jesus Encourages Us to Pray (Matthew 6:5-13) *(cont.)*

Discussion

Why is it sometimes hard to pray? Which is better—to pray at a certain time each day or to pray off and on throughout the day? Why? How can praying for other people actually help us get along with people better? What should we do when we don't feel like praying?

Bible Verse

"Do not be anxious about anything, but in everything, by prayer and petition, with thanksgiving, present your requests to God." (Philippians 4:6)

How often do you pray? Why not start the day with God by praying as soon as you wake up each morning and end the day with God by praying before you go to sleep each night? Talk to Him about anything and everything in your life. He wants to hear from you.

Craft: Prayer Request Box

Materials

- white paper
- square tissue box (empty)
- patterns on this page
- glue
- crayons or markers
- scissors

Directions

1. Copy the patterns on white paper; color and cut them out. (Each tissue box will need three heart patterns.)
2. Glue the patterns on the sides of the box. (Put the praying hands on the front side.)
3. Write your prayer requests and place them inside the box.
4. Take them out as you pray for them.

Mother's Day

Bible Story: Elisha and a Persistent Mother (2 Kings 4:8-37)

Present the Bible story as a TV news report. You will need good readers to read the parts of the reporter, Elisha, the woman, the servant, and the boy. To make the report more interesting, have the reporter use a microphone (real or homemade) as he or she talks and interviews people.

Reporter:	We have an interesting story to share with you today. I'm in the town of Shunem to talk to the people involved in this miraculous event. First, we're speaking to Elisha, a prophet of God. Can you tell us how you're involved in this story, sir?
Elisha:	Well, I first got to know the woman of Shunem when I was in town and she invited me to her home for a meal. After that, whenever I came to town I had a meal with her and her husband. Then one day they built a small room on their roof and furnished it for my visits.
Reporter:	That was very kind of them.
Elisha:	Yes, it was, and it made my work so much easier to have a comfortable place to stay. I talked to my servant about doing something for the woman to thank her. He said she wanted a son but her husband was an old man, so she probably would never have children. I knew this was what God wanted to do for her, so I told her that in a year she would give birth to a son.
Reporter:	Let's talk to Elisha's friend. How did you feel when Elisha said you would have a son?
Woman:	I was afraid at first that he didn't really mean it. But then I was thrilled! I never expected to have such a wonderful thing happen to me. I gave birth to a son about the time Elisha said I would. I knew it was God who had given me a child.
Reporter:	So everything was great after your son was born?
Woman:	For a while, but then one day my son was helping his father in the field when his head began to hurt. A servant brought him to me. I didn't know what to do, so I just held him for a long time. He died in my arms!
Reporter:	What did you do?
Woman:	I told my husband to send one of the servants to me with a donkey. I laid my dead son on the bed in Elisha's room; then I got on the donkey and the servant and I went off to find Elisha.
Reporter:	Where did she find you, Elisha?
Elisha:	I was at Mount Carmel. I saw her coming and sent my servant to find out what she wanted.
Woman:	I told his servant everything was all right. It wasn't, but I wanted to speak directly to Elisha.
Reporter:	Can you tell us more, Gehazi?
Servant:	Well, she knelt down at Elisha's feet. I didn't think she should be doing that, so I started to push her away, but my master told me to leave her alone.

(continued on next page)

Mother's Day

Bible Story: Elisha and a Persistent Mother (2 Kings 4:8-37) *(cont.)*

Elisha:	She told me what had happened, so I sent my servant to hurry to her home and lay my staff on the boy's face. I thought it might revive him.
Servant:	But it didn't work.
Woman:	I refused to leave Elisha until he came and healed my son himself.
Elisha:	When I reached the house, I found the boy lying on my bed. He was dead. I shut the door and prayed to the Lord. He brought life back into her son's body.
Reporter:	Is this your son, Ma'am?
Woman:	Yes. Tell him what happened to you, son.
Boy:	I don't really know what happened. I was in a deep, deep sleep when suddenly I woke up and began sneezing! I looked up and there was Elisha standing over me.
Elisha:	I told my servant to bring the boy's mother to my room. She came in and bowed at my feet, then took her son and left. Of course, I wasn't the one who gave the boy back his life. God did it.
Reporter:	Thank you all for talking with us today to share this wonderful story. That's our report for today. Thanks for being with us.

Discussion

Do you think this mother had faith in God? How did she show her faith? How did she show her love for her son? How does your mother show she loves you?

Bible Verse

"As a mother comforts her child, so will I comfort you . . . ."
(Isaiah 66:13)

How does your mother comfort you when you're sick or hurt or sad? How do you think God comforts us?

Thanks, Mom for all you do!

Finished Product

Craft: Teacup Magnet

Materials

- magnet
- glue
- tea bag
- scissors
- crayons or markers
- white cardstock
- patterns on page 45
- flower patterns from page 50 (or pre-cut foam flowers found at local craft stores)

Mother's Day

Craft: Teacup Magnet *(cont.)*

Directions

1. Copy the patterns on white cardstock. Color and cut them out.
2. Glue the flowers on the cup.
3. Glue the edges of the two teacup patterns together to form a pocket. Then glue the cup to the saucer.
4. Glue a magnet on the back of the cup and place a tea bag inside.
5. Give the magnet to Mom.

"As a mother comforts her child, so will I comfort you . . . ."
(Isaiah 66:13)

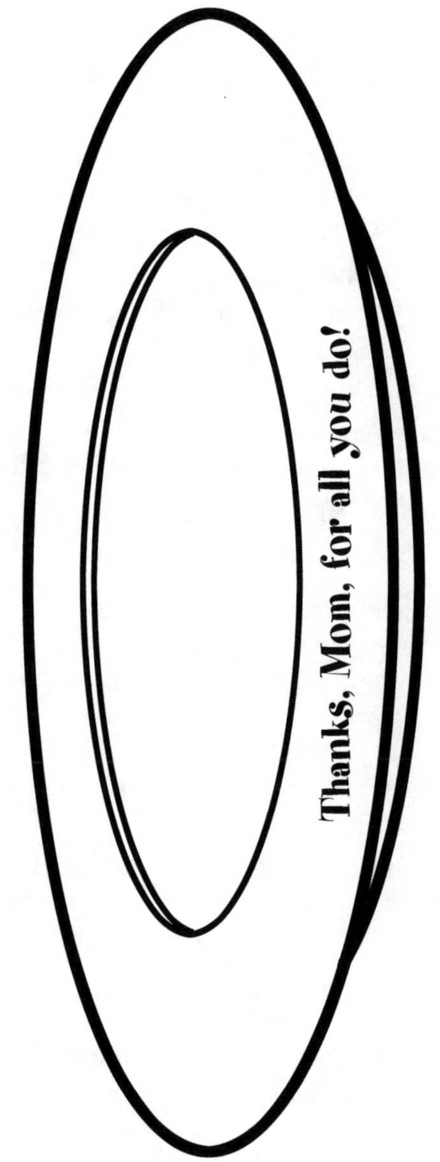
Thanks, Mom, for all you do!

Cut out center.

Mother's Day

Bible Story: Jesus and His Mother (Luke 2:41-52; selected New Testament Scriptures)

Say this action rhyme for your students with the actions; then have them say it with you.

Mary was a young girl God chose specially
(*Point toward heaven.*)

To be the mother of His Son
who died for you and me.
(*Stretch out arms in the shape of a cross.*)

She loved the Lord and taught her son
to read God's Word and pray.
(*Open hands like an open Bible;*
then fold hands in prayer.)

He always did what Mary said;
He never disobeyed.
(*Shake head yes, then no.*)

When He was twelve,
His parents took Him to Jerusalem.
(*Point to a distant place.*)

They visited the temple
and Jesus went with them.
(*Walk in place and look around.*)

On the way back home,
they could not find Him anywhere!
(*Look all around.*)

They went back to the temple
and finally found Him there.
(*Put hands on hips and sigh as if in relief.*)

He was with the teachers
asking questions of them all.
(*Put finger on top of head as if thinking hard.*)

Jesus stopped and looked up
when He heard His mother call,
(*Look down; then look up with a smile.*)

"Why have you treated us like this?
We thought we had lost You!"
(*Shake index finger as if scolding.*)

"Didn't you know," Jesus said,
"that this is what I'd do?"
(*Raise hands and shrug shoulders*
as if asking a question.)

They went back home
where Jesus honored Mary as He should.
(*Put hand over heart.*)

He always was obedient, patient, kind, and good.
(*Count off character traits on your fingers.*)

Even when He grew up and became a man,
(*Hold hand above your head to show height.*)

Jesus honored Mary
because that was God's plan.
(*Point toward heaven.*)

Right before He died,
Jesus asked His good friend John
(*Clasp hands.*)

To take care of Mary,
he would become like a son.
(*Hold out hands, then move them close together.*)

Jesus honored Mary and He loved her too.
(*Cross hands over heart.*)

Honoring our mothers
is what God wants us to do.
(*Point toward heaven.*)

Discussion

What are some reasons you are thankful for your mom? What are some things your mom does for you? How often do you thank her for being a great mom? Is once a year on Mother's Day enough? How often do you thank God for giving your mom to you? How can you show respect for your mom? Does obedience have anything to do with respect?

Bible Verse

"Honor your father and your mother." (Exodus 20:12a) What does it mean to "honor" your mother? What are some ways you can do that? (Encourage children to think of practical ideas, more than giving Mom a gift or card.)

Mother's Day

Craft: Mother's Day Card

Materials

- cardstock
- pattern below
- markers or crayons

Directions

1. Cover up the top half of this page and copy the whole page onto cardstock.
2. Color the picture.
3. Fold the page to make a card.
4. Flip it open and write a message to your mom inside.

Variation: Glue real flowers, sequins, or glitter to the card.

For Mom

Thank you for loving me!

"Honor your father and your mother."

(Exodus 20:12a)

Mother's Day

Bible Story: Hannah and Samuel (1 Samuel 1:1-2:11)

Let students spread out around the room and quietly pantomime the story as you tell it. To get them started suggest that they act out walking to the tabernacle, crying, praying, and rocking a baby.

Elkanah was a godly man who went on a trip every year to the tabernacle to worship God. Hannah, his wife, was very sad because she had no children. Elkanah tried to cheer her up and tell Hannah it was okay, but she was too downhearted to listen to him. She was so sad, she cried and couldn't eat.

One day at the tabernacle, Hannah prayed, crying as she silently spoke to God. "O Lord Almighty," she said, "if you will only give me a son, I will give him to You, to serve You." Eli the priest saw her crying and moving her lips. He did not realize she was praying; he thought she had been drinking too much. He scolded her, but she explained that she had been praying that God would give her a son.

"Go in peace," Eli told her, "and may the God of Israel grant you what you have asked of Him."

The Lord blessed Hannah and Elkanah with a son and she named him Samuel. Hannah did not go with her husband when he went to the tabernacle that year, but stayed home with her baby. She loved and cared for her son and taught him to love God. Then when Samuel was three years old, Hannah went to the tabernacle with Elkanah and they took Samuel with them. Hannah took little Samuel to Eli the priest. "I give him to the Lord," she said. "For his whole life he will be given over to the Lord."

It was very hard for Hannah to give up the son she loved so much, but she had promised God. Samuel lived with Eli and helped him. Hannah only saw him once a year when she and Elkanah went to worship at the tabernacle. She always made a new robe for her son to wear and took it to him on their yearly visit. In the short time Samuel had lived at home with his mother, she had taught him to love God and serve Him. Samuel grew up to be one of the greatest prophets of God.

Discussion

Why does your mom do so much for you? Why does she love you? What is the best way for you to show your mom you love her? *(Mothers do not just say they love us; they demonstrate it in all the things they do for us. We should do the same.)*

Bible Verse

"Love is patient, love is kind. . . . Love never fails. . . ." (1 Corinthians 13:4a, 8a)

God wants us to love our moms and do what they say. Even when you are all grown up, you should never "forsake" or stop following what your mom taught you.

Mother's Day

Craft: Mother's Day Photo Frame

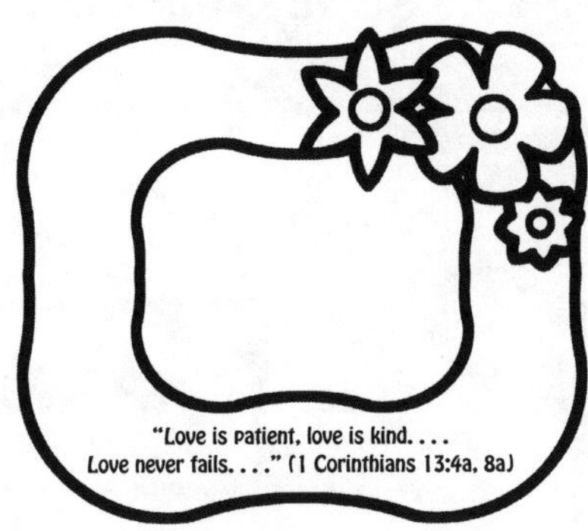

Finished Product

Materials

- patterns on pages 49 and 50
- crayons or markers
- magnetic strip *(optional)*
- glue and tape
- cardstock
- scissors

Directions

1. Copy the patterns on cardstock. Color the patterns and cut them out.
2. Decorate the flowers and glue them to the frame.
3. Cut out the center of the frame.
4. Tape a picture to the back of each frame.
5. Glue a magnetic strip on back of each picture frame, or assemble the A-frame stand on page 50 to hold the frame.
6. Have students give the completed frames to their moms.

Variation: Use pre-cut foam flowers found at local craft supply stores.

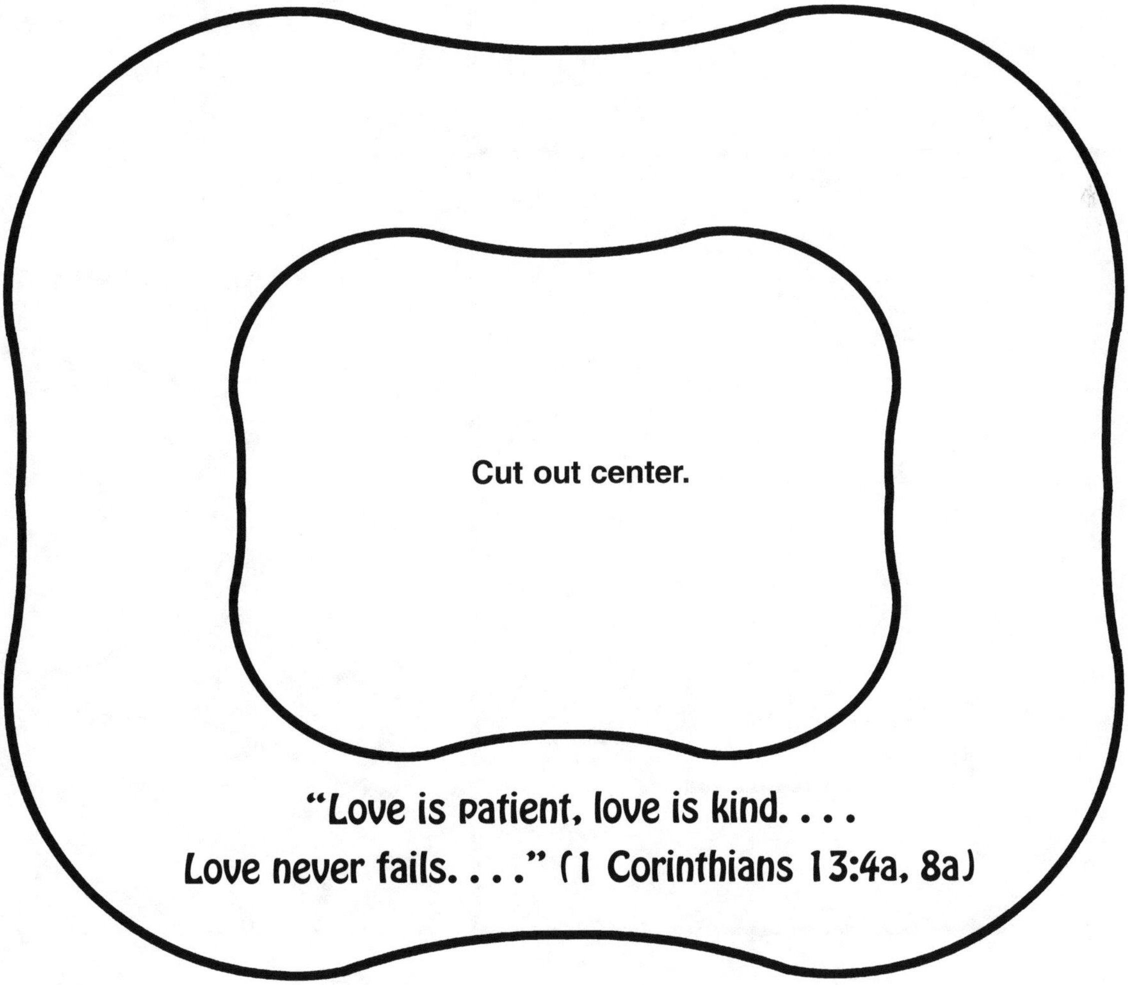

Cut out center.

**"Love is patient, love is kind. . . .
Love never fails. . . ." (1 Corinthians 13:4a, 8a)**

Mother's Day

A-Frame Stand (Attach to back of pictures.)

Tape strip here.

Finished Product

Fold line.

Tape strip here.

Tape to A-Frame.

Fold line.

Fold line.

Tape to A-Frame.

Flower Patterns

Ascension Day

Bible Story: Jesus Goes Back to Heaven (Acts 1:1-11)

Tell the Bible story by singing the song; then have students sing it with you.

(*Tune:* "I Will Make You Fishers of Men")

Jesus died, but didn't stay dead, didn't stay dead, didn't stay dead.

Jesus died, but didn't stay dead. For He rose again.

Jesus rose again; yes He rose again.

Jesus died, but didn't stay dead. For He rose again.

He spent forty days with His friends, teaching His friends, encouraging them.

He spent forty days with His friends, then He went away.

Jesus went away; yes He went away.

He spent forty days with His friends, then He went away.

He went up to heaven that day, and they all watched Him go away.

He went up to heaven that day right before their eyes.

Right before their eyes, disappeared from sight.

He went up to heaven that day right before their eyes.

Then two angels said to His friends, "He will return; it's not the end."

Then two angels said to His friends, "He'll return one day.

He'll return one day as He went away."

Then two angels said to His friends, "He'll return one day."

Discussion

What do you think the angels meant when they said Jesus would one day come back the same way He went to heaven? When will Jesus return? What did Jesus tell His friends He wanted them to do until He returned? (Read Acts 1:8 to find out.)

Bible Verse

"You heard me say, 'I am going away and I am coming back to you.'" (John 14:28a)

Before He was arrested and crucified, Jesus told His disciples that He was going to leave them, but He would return. They did not understand Him. When will He come back? How can we be ready to meet Jesus when He returns?

Ascension Day

Craft: Jesus' Ascension Picture

Materials

- patterns on pages 52 and 53
- blue construction paper
- yarn or twine
- glue
- hole punch
- cardstock
- crayons or markers
- tape
- scissors

Directions

1. Copy the patterns on cardstock for durability and color them.
2. Cut out all patterns and glue all the patterns on a sheet of blue construction paper, except the pattern of Jesus. Do not glue the bottom of the clouds.
3. Tape yarn or twine to the back of the Jesus figure.
4. Punch holes in the top and bottom of the blue sheet. Knot the yarn or twine at the top and bottom, using a slightly longer piece than the length of the paper.
5. Pull the yarn or twine up and down to make Jesus disappear into the clouds.

Finished Product

**"You heard me say,
'I am going away and
I am coming back to you.'"
(John 14:28a)**

Background Pattern

Craft: Jesus' Ascension Picture *(cont.)*

Cloud Patterns

Jesus Pattern

Memorial Day

Bible Story: Conquering Jericho (Joshua 6)

Follow the directions and have students walk around the room, as if marching around Jericho, as you tell the story.

God had brought His people to the Promised Land, but there were ungodly, idol-worshiping people living there. God planned for His people, led by Joshua, to conquer all the people so they could live freely in the land. Their first big challenge was the city of Jericho. The large city was completely surrounded by huge walls, keeping out the Israelites. How would they conquer the city if they could not even get into it? God told Joshua exactly what to do, and Joshua told his people.

God's plan was for the people to silently march once around the city every day for six days. Then on the seventh day, the people were to march around seven times. On the seventh time around the priests would blow a loud blast on their trumpets and the people would shout out loud. God would make the city wall collapse, and the people could go in and fight to conquer the city.

Joshua and the people did exactly what God said. (*Have students line up and march silently around, the room; then sit down. Do this six times. Then have them march around the room seven times. During the seventh time around, choose a student to make a noise like a trumpet; then let everyone shout.*) And God did what he had promised. The huge wall fell down and the people ran in and conquered Jericho.

Over and over again, God fought for His people, helping them defeat their enemies so they could finally live in freedom. When Joshua was an old man, his people lived at peace in the Promised Land. He reminded them that their freedom was from God. They could never have conquered the land on their own. The Israelite army had won many battles because God had fought for them. The people needed to be thankful to the soldiers who had fought for them, but also to God for giving them victory over their enemies.

Discussion

Why do you think God chose such an unusual way to conquer Jericho? How should we pray for soldiers fighting around the world today?

Bible Verse

"The Lord your God fights for you, just as he promised." (Joshua 23:10b)

How does God fight for us today? How can we show our thanks to Him?

Memorial Day

Craft: Memorial Day Wind Sock

Materials

- patterns on pages 55 and 56
- crayons or markers
- string or yarn
- hole punch
- scissors
- cardstock
- 1- to 2-inch wide ribbon
- stapler or tape
- glue

Finished Product

Directions

1. Copy the patterns on cardstock. Make two copies of page 56.
2. Color and cut them out.
3. With the two patterns from page 56, staple or tape two of the ends together. Form into a tube and staple or tape together.
4. Have the children glue the Freedom Isn't Free! pattern on the wind sock.
5. Cut strips of ribbon in various lengths and staple them to the points of the wind sock.
6. Punch four to five holes around the top. Insert yarn or string in each one of the holes, securing them at the base and pulling them together at the middle. Tie them to hang the wind sock.

Freedom Isn't Free! Pattern

Freedom Isn't Free!

"The Lord your God fights for you, just as he promised."

(Joshua 23:10b)

Craft: Memorial Day Wind Sock *(cont.)*

Wind Sock Pattern

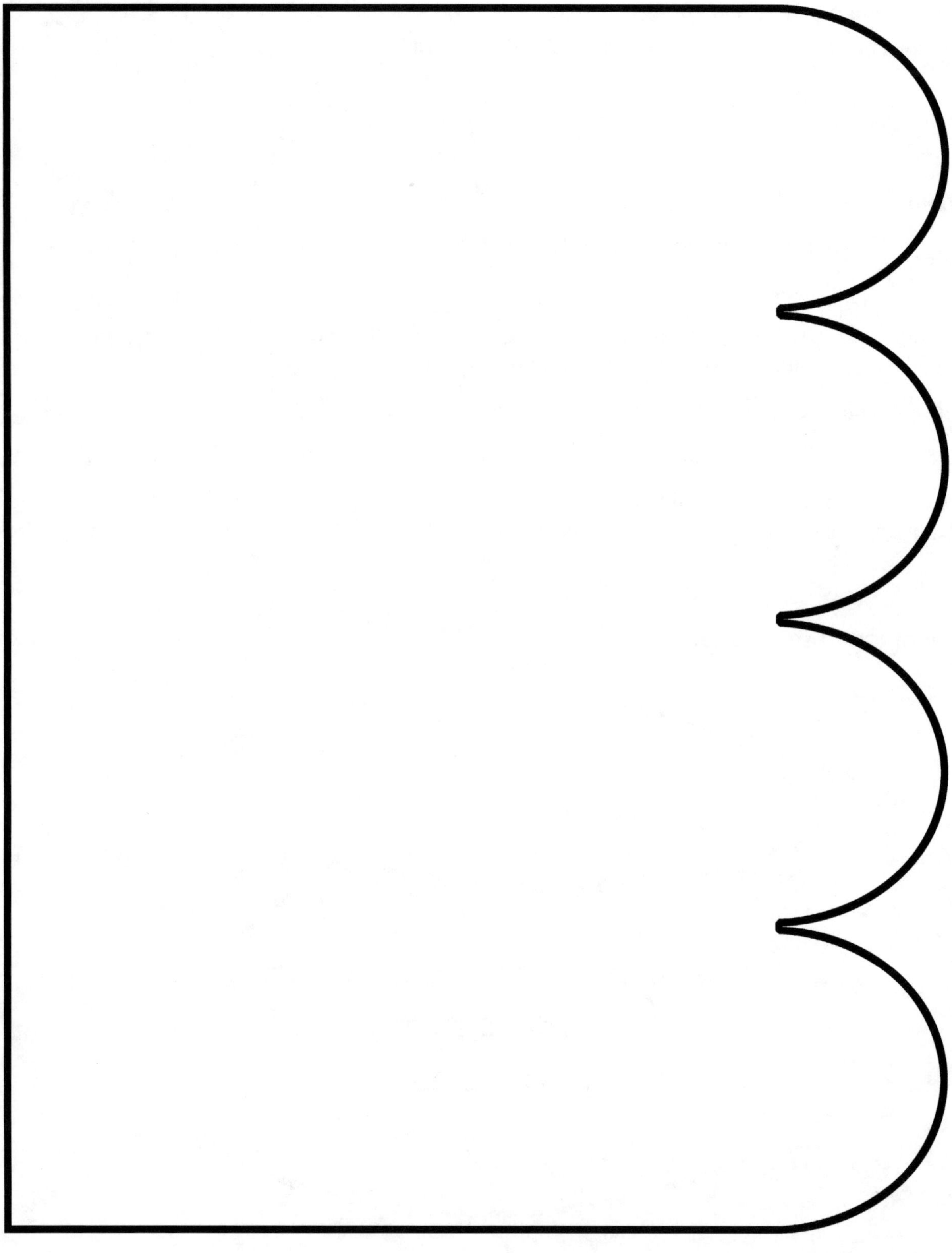

Memorial Day

Bible Story: David's Fighting Men (2 Samuel 23:8-23)

As you talk about David's fighting men, print each name on the board. Have students repeat them after you.

David spent most of his life fighting Israel's enemies. He won most battles, but not all. He didn't have to fight alone but had an army of strong, loyal soldiers who fought for him, many to their deaths.

<u>Josheb</u> once fought and defeated 800 men, all at one encounter.

<u>Eleazar</u> fought in a battle with David against the Philistines. Most of the army retreated, but Eleazar stayed and fought so long and so hard, at the end of the battle he couldn't let go of his sword.

<u>Shammah</u> fought the Philistines, but many of his fellow soldiers ran away. Not Shammah! He stood in the middle of a field and struck Philistines down as they attacked him.

<u>Abishai</u> defeated 300 men with his spear and became a commander in the army.

<u>Benaiah</u> struck down two dozen Moabites. He went down into a pit on a snowy day and killed a lion. Benaiah struck down a huge Egyptian with a club, snatching the man's spear from him.

During a lull in a battle with the Philistines one day, David said he wished he could have a drink of water from the well near the gate of Bethlehem, his hometown. Three of his faithful soldiers sneaked out of camp, broke through the Philistine guard, and dipped water from the well. Then they carried it back to their commander in chief. David was overwhelmed at what the men had done. He couldn't bring himself to drink the water, but poured it out as an offering to the Lord. He felt unworthy to drink water that his men had risked their lives to get, but he was thankful to them for wanting to help him.

David knew it was God who gave him strong and loyal soldiers who fought as hard as they could, and it was God who gave them victory over their enemies. David honored his soldiers as well as God.

Discussion

Do you know soldiers who have fought for America or are fighting somewhere now? (*Let students share the names of soldiers they know.*) Let us thank God for them and all the men and women who fight for freedom and sometimes give their lives for our country.

Bible Verse

"I thank my God every time I remember you." (Philippians 1:3)

How can you show your thanks for people who have fought and died so you could live in a free land?

Memorial Day

Craft: Patriotic Pin

Materials

- 1" wooden or heavy cardboard square
- white star (from cardstock or button)
- dark blue paint and paint brush
- glue
- black fine-tip marker
- red fabric
- safety pin or button pin
- scissors

Directions

1. Paint the square blue. Let dry.
2. Cut a one-inch wide piece of fabric about two to three inches long. Glue it to the back of the square so that the fabric hangs below the square.
3. After the glue dries, cut small slits up the fabric to the square to represent the flag's stripes.
4. Neatly print the words of Philippians 1:3 on the strips: "I thank my God every time I remember you."
5. Glue a star on the square.
6. Glue a pin on the back of the square.
7. Give the pin to someone you know who has served in America's military.

Variation: Use a wooden or craft foam star.

Finished Product

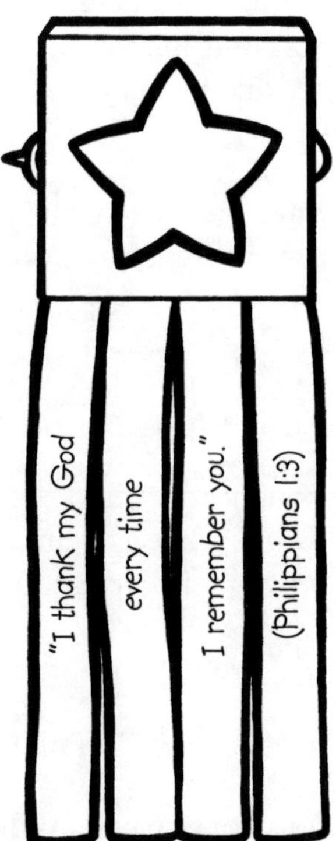

Flag Day

Bible Story: Remembering God's Goodness (Joshua 3:1-4:18)

Bring a large box and two poles to class. Choose four students to carry the box by holding the poles on their shoulders. As you tell the story, walk around the room behind the four box carriers. Have students follow you. The box represents the Ark of the Covenant. Pretend to cross the river together.

Joshua and the Israelites were ready to enter the Promised Land. All they had to do was go across the Jordan River and they would be there! But the river was in a flood stage, and it would be dangerous to try to go across. Even strong swimmers might be swept away by the churning water. Then God told Joshua what to do. The priests were to carry the Ark of the Covenant into the river and stop right in the middle. The priests did what God said. As soon as their feet touched the water, the water from upstream stopped flowing. They walked to the middle of the river on dry ground. The Israelites crossed over the river without even getting their feet wet!

Then Joshua chose twelve men to each pick up a stone from the middle of the river where the priests were standing and carry it to the other side of the river. They put the twelve stones on the ground near the place they would camp that night. Joshua piled up the stones to make a memorial to remind the people what God had done for them there.

After all the people had crossed the river, the priests walked the rest of the way across, carrying the Ark of the Covenant. No sooner had they stepped onto the river bank than the water in the river began flowing again.

"In the future when your descendants ask their fathers, 'What do these stones mean?' tell them what God did for us here today," Joshua said to the people.

Discussion

Ask students to name some American symbols—things that stand for freedom. (eagle, flag, memorials such as the Washington Monument and the Jefferson Memorial, etc.) Then ask them to tell what they love and enjoy most about America. Make sure each student has a chance to express an opinion. Pray together, thanking God for all the ways He has blessed America.

Bible Verse

"So if the Son sets you free, you will be free indeed." (John 8:36)

As Americans, we have many, many freedoms we can remember and for which we thank God. Our flag and other American symbols remind us to be thankful for what He has given us.

Flag Day

Craft: Pocket Flag

Materials

- red, white, and blue fabric
- magnetic strips
- needle and thread *(optional)*
- fabric glue
- cards on pages 61 and 62
- scissors

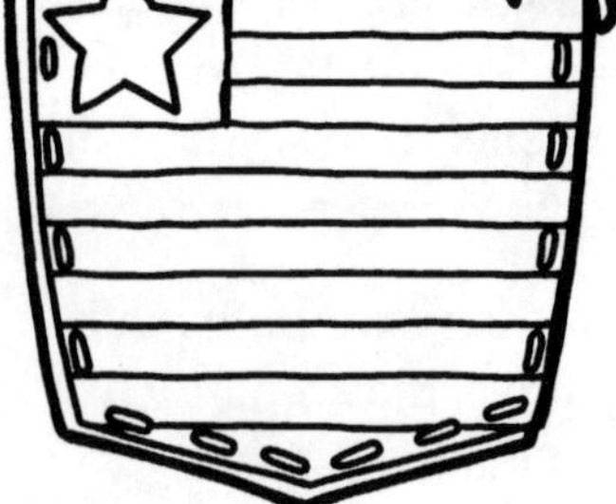

Finished Product

Directions

1. Cut two copies of the pattern below from blue fabric and one copy of the star on white fabric.
2. Glue or stitch the pocket edges together, leaving the top open.
3. Cut strips of red cloth and glue them on like the stripes of the flag.
4. Cut a magnetic strip the width of the top of the pocket and attach it to the back. Also, cut a magnetic strip to place on the bottom.
5. Cut out the cards on pages 61 and 62. Store the freedom verses in the pocket after memorizing them. Use the blank cards to write down favorite verses.

Variation: Use a real cloth jean back pocket (do not cut the pocket off the jeans, cut both the pocket and the jean itself) to make the pocket design and a craft foam star to put on it. Or, use colored paper or cardstock for the project.

Pocket Pattern

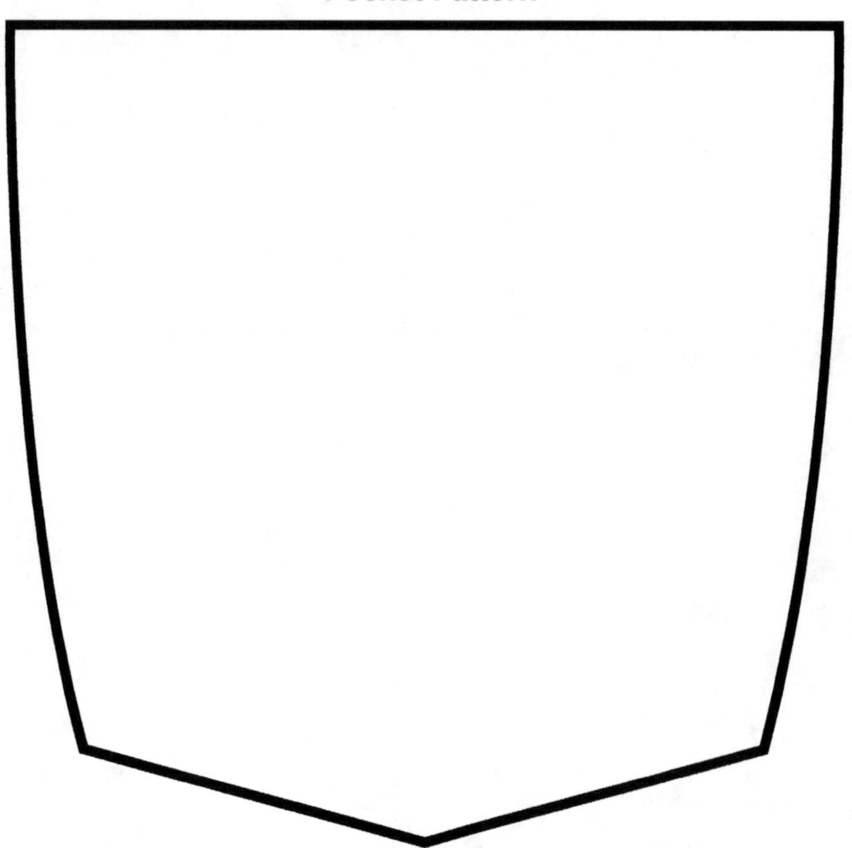

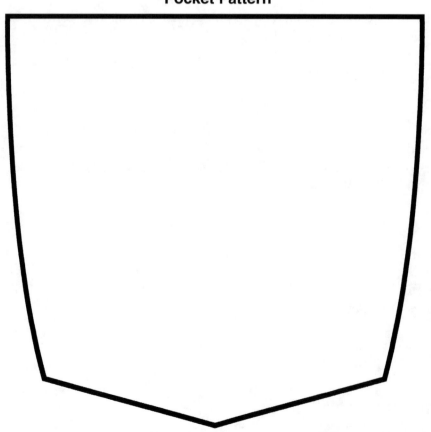

Star Pattern

Flag Day

Freedom Verse Cards

"So if the Son sets you free, you will be free indeed."

John 8:36

"It is for freedom that Christ has set us free."

Galatians 5:1a

"I will walk about in freedom, for I have sought out your precepts."

Psalm 119:45

"If my people, who are called by my name, will humble themselves and pray and seek my face and turn from their wicked ways, then will I hear from heaven and will forgive their sin and will heal their land."

2 Chronicles 7:14

Flag Day

Freedom Verse Cards

"Observe the commands of the Lord your God, walking in his ways and revering him. For the Lord your God is bringing you into a good land."

Deuteronomy 8:6–7a

Flag Day

Craft: Patriotic Door Swag

Finished Product

Materials

- star patterns below
- paint (red, white, and blue)
- red, white and blue fabric
- tagboard
- yarn or jute rope
- scissors and hole punch

Directions

1. Copy the patterns onto tagboard and cut out the stars. You will need several stars of different sizes.
2. Paint the stars red, white, and blue. (The star with the words on it should be white. As an option, write freedom verses from pages 61 and 62 on the stars.)
3. Punch a hole in the top of each star. Thread yarn or jute into the holes. (Or tape the yarn or jute to the backs of the stars.)
4. Gather the strings and tie them in a knot at the top. Hang the swag on a door.

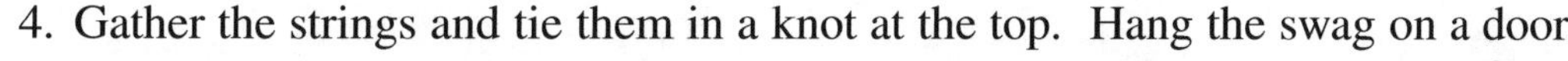

Star Patterns

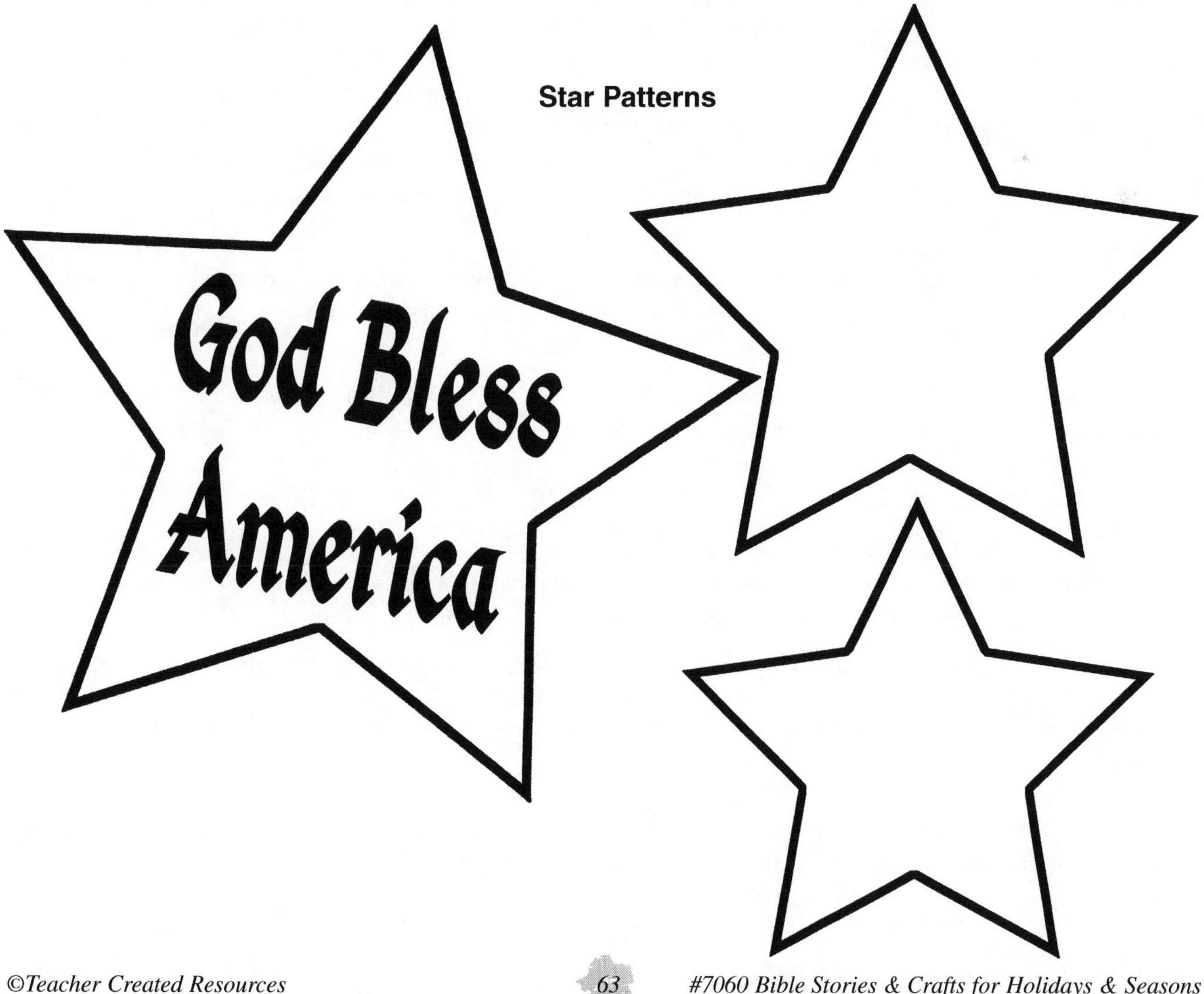

God Bless America

Father's Day

Bible Story: David and Solomon (1 Kings 2:1-12; 3:1-15)

Print Solomon's name vertically on the board. As you tell the story, create a word acrostic, writing words on his name, that tell what David's advice was to his son as shown below.

	S	HOW YOURSELF A MAN
	O	BEY GOD
W A	**L**	K IN HIS WAYS
USE WISD	**O**	M
KEEP HIS COM	**M**	ANDS
BE STR	**O**	NG
BE KI	**N**	D

David was King of Israel for forty years, and he grew to be an old man. It was time for his son Solomon to become the king. Before he died, David gave his son some advice on how to be a good king. David was the greatest king Israel ever had, so he knew what he was talking about. "Show yourself a man," David told Solomon. A king had to be an honest and upright man if he wanted to lead his people well. "Be strong," David said. A king had to be a strong leader, and David knew there was only one way to be the strong leader Israel needed. "Observe what the Lord your God requires," David advised Solomon. That simply means obey God. David knew that Solomon would need help to be a good king, and God was the best one to help him.

"Keep His commands," David went on. "Walk in His ways." Solomon must not try to go his own way, or he would fail. David also advised him to use wisdom in whatever he did and to be kind. A king had great power, but he should not abuse his power by mistreating people. He must be fair and just to everyone.

Not long after this, David died and Solomon became king. One night God spoke to Solomon in a dream. "Ask for whatever you want me to give you," God said to him. Wow! This was Solomon's chance to ask for the thing he wanted most! What would it be—great wealth? power? fame? popularity?

Solomon proved that he had listened to David and was following his advice. He asked God to give him wisdom so he could be a good king. God was so pleased with Solomon's request, He promised to give him not only great wisdom, but also great riches and honor.

Solomon became known as the wisest and wealthiest king Israel ever had. He did what his father had told him to do, and God blessed him.

Discussion

Why do you think children should listen to their fathers' instruction and advice? Why does your father know more than you do about most things? The Bible refers to God as our Heavenly Father. Do you listen to His instructions and do what He says?

Father's Day

Bible Story: David and Solomon (1 Kings 2:1-12; 3:1-15) *(cont.)*

Bible Verse

"A wise son heeds his father's instruction." (Proverbs 13:1a)

"Heeds" means *listens and obeys*. The best way to honor your father on Father's Day and every day is to listen to what he tells you and to obey.

Craft: Sporty Picture Frame

Materials

- white cardstock
- red marker
- A-Frame Stand on page 50
- glue and tape
- photo of child
- scissors

Directions

1. Copy the ball pattern on cardstock and cut it out.
2. Cut out the center for a picture.
3. Use a red marker to draw over the stitches on the ball.
4. Tape your photo at the back of the ball. Attach the ball to the A-Frame stand.

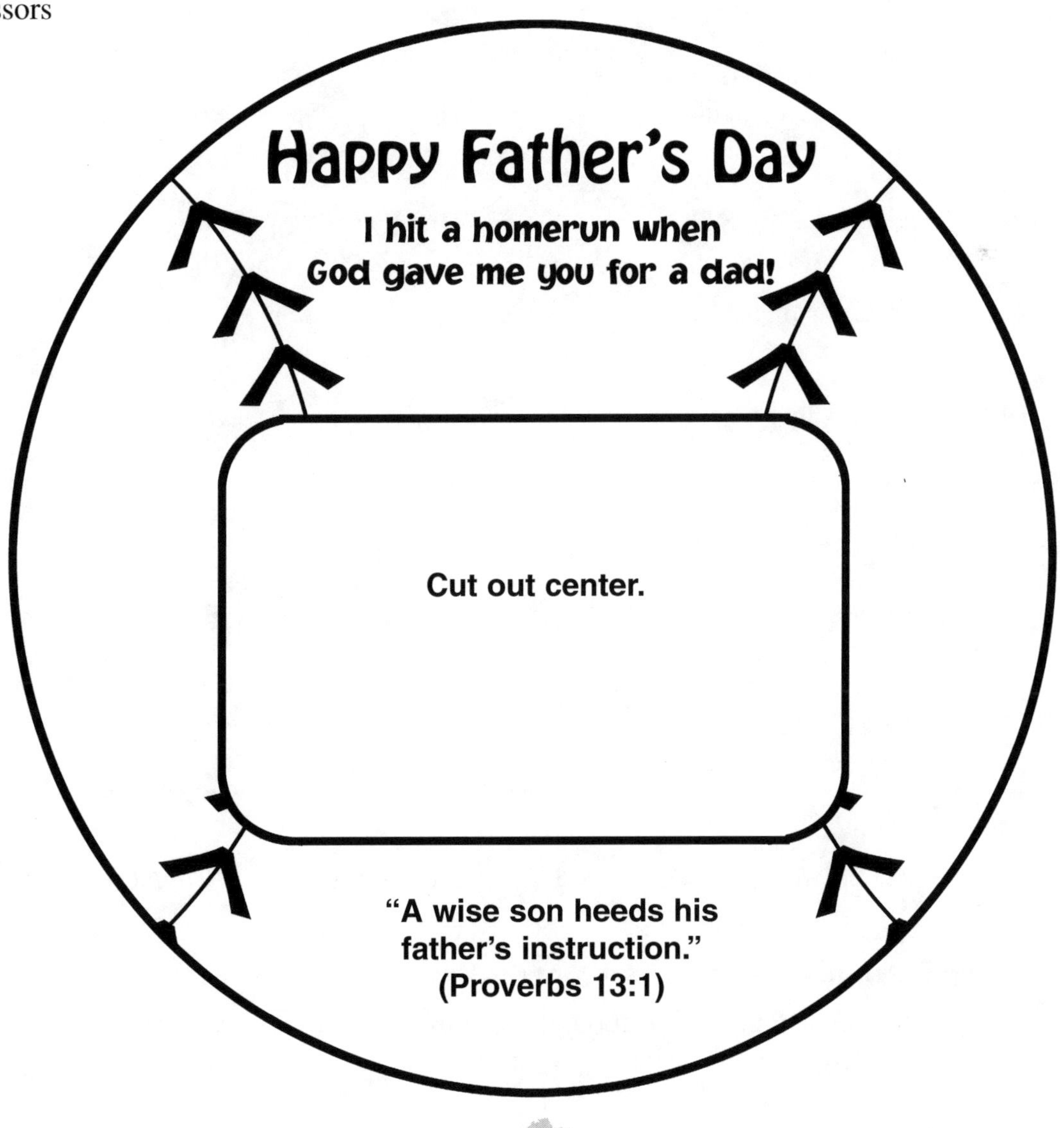

Happy Father's Day

I hit a homerun when God gave me you for a dad!

Cut out center.

"A wise son heeds his father's instruction." (Proverbs 13:1)

Father's Day

Bible Story: Joseph Helps Jacob (Genesis 37; 45-46)

Say the echo action rhyme, encouraging students to repeat each line after you and copy your actions.

Jacob had twelve sons, but his favorite was little Joe.	(*Count to* twelve *on your fingers, then hold up one.*)
He gave him a special coat because he loved him so.	(*Hold out arms as if modeling coat.*)
The brothers were jealous and treated Joseph so badly.	(*Fold arms and look angry.*)
They said that he had died, and Jacob was very sad.	(*Pretend to cry.*)
But Joseph wasn't dead; he was living in Egypt land.	(*Point far away.*)
Things looked bad for him, but it was all God's plan.	(*Point toward heaven.*)
Joseph trusted God, worked hard, and did not complain.	(*Cross hands over heart.*)
And one day Pharaoh put him in charge of storing Egypt's grain.	(*Hold out arms as if proud of what you've done.*)
His brothers came to Egypt to buy grain and found their brother.	(*Hold hands up to cheeks and look shocked.*)
Joseph forgave them all and they welcomed one another.	(*Hug yourself.*)
"Go home and get my father and your families," he said.	(*Point far away.*)
"Tell him that his little Joe is alive—not dead!"	(*Raise arms over head and jump.*)
Jacob and his family traveled to that place.	(*Walk in place.*)
Joseph went to meet him with a big smile on his face.	(*Grin big.*)
Joseph took care of them all; so glad to have them there.	(*Spread out arms as if indicating a large group.*)
He helped his father every day to show how much he cared.	(*Place hand over heart.*)

Discussion

What do you love most about your dad? (*Let every student share his or her thoughts.*)

Bible Verse

" . . . A wise son brings joy to his father. . . ." (Proverbs 10:1a)

How did Joseph bring joy to his father? It's good to give gifts and cards on Father's Day, but what do you think your dad would like even more than a gift or card?

Father's Day

Craft: Dad's Helper Wheel

Finished Product

Materials

- white cardstock
- markers or crayons
- patterns on pages 67–69
- glue
- brad fastener
- scissors

Directions

1. Copy the patterns on pages 67–69 on cardstock.
2. Cut out the patterns and color.
3. Cut out the window on the front of the the Dad's Helper Wheel on page 68.
4. Glue the tools to the front of the wheel.
5. Align the two wheels so that the chore can be seen in the window opening.
6. Poke a brad fastener in the middle to hold the two wheels together.
7. Give it to dad for Father's Day.

Tool Patterns

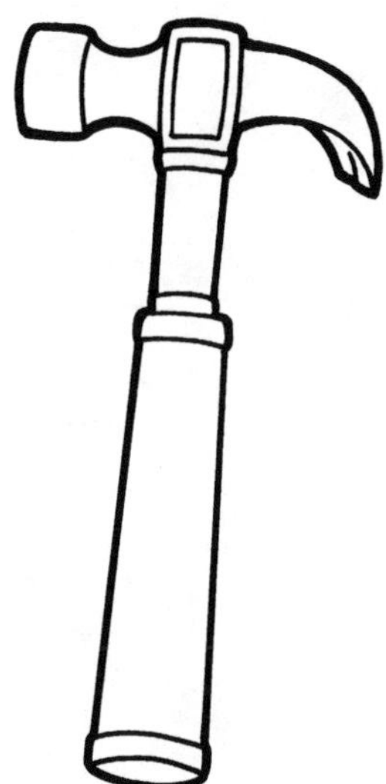

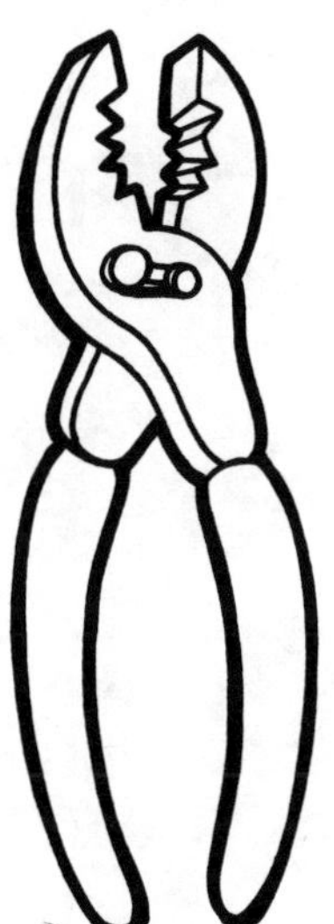

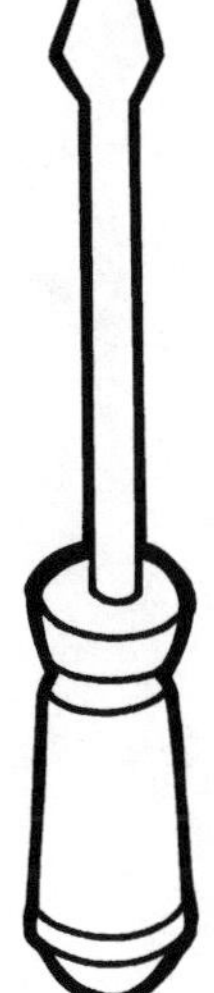

Craft: Dad's Helper Wheel *(cont.)*

Dad's Helper Wheel (Front)

DAD'S
Helper Wheel

A wise son [or daughter] brings joy to his [or her] father.

(Proverbs 10:1a)

Craft: Dad's Helper Wheel *(cont.)*

Dad's Helper Wheel (Back)

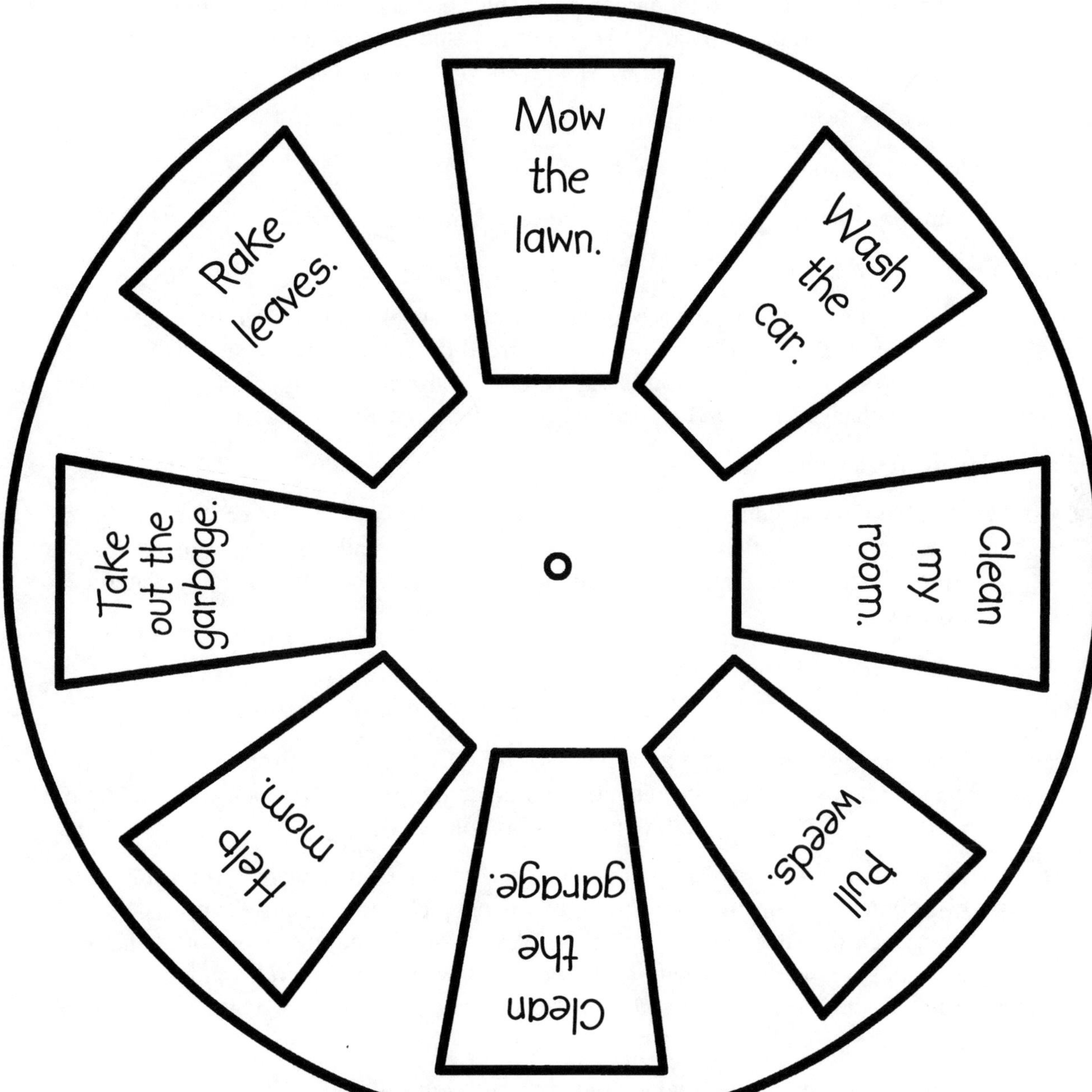

Mow the lawn.

Wash the car.

Clean my room.

Pull weeds.

Clean the garage.

Help mom.

Take out the garbage.

Rake leaves.

Father's Day

Bible Story: Jethro Advises Moses (Exodus 18)

Choose two students to read the parts of Jethro and Moses. You read the part of the narrator in this skit. To make it more realistic, have the two students dress in robes and wear Bible-time head coverings.

Narrator:	Moses was a great leader of the Israelites. God had chosen him to lead the people out of Egypt and take them across the desert to the Promised Land. But there was so much to do! Moses always seemed to be busy helping the people. It was exhausting! Then one day his father-in-law, Jethro, came to visit him. Moses had been separated from his own father since Pharaoh's daughter had adopted him as a child in Egypt. He had been raised in the palace, so his father wasn't around to advise him. But his wife's father was like a father to Moses, so Moses was glad to see him.
Moses:	Welcome, Father! It is good to see you.
Jethro:	Moses, my son, how are you?
Moses:	I am fine, but very busy. The work never seems to get done.
Jethro:	Tell me what has been happening to you.
Moses:	Well, you heard, I am sure, about the terrible plagues God brought on Egypt. Pharaoh was a hard-hearted man, but he finally agreed to let us leave his land. He did not want to let us go, but it was the only way he knew to make the plagues stop. Then after we left, he changed his mind and came riding after us with his huge army!
Jethro:	How frightening!
Moses:	Yes, but God saved us by creating a path across the sea for us to cross over. When Pharaoh's soldiers tried to follow, God closed up the path and they were swept away. Since then, God has been with us all along the way, providing food and water and protecting us.
Jethro:	Praise God! He is so great!
Moses:	Yes, He is.
Narrator:	The next day Moses acted as a judge for the people all day. From morning until evening he listened to their disputes and made judgments for them. He told them what God's Law said. Later, Jethro spoke to his son-in-law.
Jethro:	Moses, why are you wearing yourself out with this kind of work? You cannot do everything by yourself! You should be the people's representative before God and bring their disputes to Him. But choose trustworthy men to be your officials. Assign a certain number of people to each one, and have the men serve as judges. They can bring the difficult cases to you. The people will still be satisfied, and you'll be able to stand the strain of all your other work.
Moses:	Thank you, Father; that's good advice. I will do what you say right away.
Narrator:	Moses followed Jethro's wise advice, and it worked fine. Moses could relax a little.

Father's Day

Bible Story: Jethro Advises Moses (Exodus 18) *(cont.)*

Discussion

Moses did not have his father around to give him advice, but Jethro was like a father to him. Do you listen to your father when he gives you advice? With what kinds of things do you ask him to help you? Why do you trust what he says?

Bible Verse

"Listen to your father, who gave you life. . . ." (Proverbs 23:22a)

You have two fathers who gave you life—your human father and your Heavenly Father. God wants you to listen to both of them. How can you listen to your Heavenly Father's teaching and advice?

Craft: Candy Airplane

Materials

- two circular candies with holes in the middle
- package of gum
- small rectangular solid candy
- small rubber band
- Bible verse strip

Directions

1. Thread the rubber band between the holes of the circular candies.
2. Place the rectangular solid candy between the circular candies and rest the gum on top. Stretch the rubber band around the gum to secure.

Finished Product

3. Slip the Bible verse strip between the rubber bands on top of the gum package.

Bible Verse Strip

Having you for a dad
is a special treat!
"Listen to your father, who gave you life."
(Proverbs 23:22a)

Independence Day

Bible Story: Bible Celebrations (Selected Old Testament passages)

List the names of the Bible festivals on the board as you talk about them. Then review them with a few questions at the end.

In Old Testament times, God encouraged His people to celebrate special occasions, called *festivals*. There were many festivals, but three main ones.

There was the Feast of the Passover (Deuteronomy 16:1–8), a time to remember when God rescued His people from slavery in Egypt. For this festival, each family was to cook a lamb and eat it with flat bread and bitter herbs. This food reminded them of the night when God passed over their homes, but took the life of the oldest son in every Egyptian family. It was this event that made Pharaoh let them leave Egypt. Passover was a time for people to think of God's love and to thank Him for His protection.

Pentecost (Exodus 23:16) was also called the Feast of Harvest. It was celebrated seven weeks after Passover. On this day no work was to be done, and special offerings were made to God. It was an occasion for rejoicing and praising God for good crops.

The Feast of Tabernacles (Deuteronomy 16:13–15) was a seven-day celebration which people observed by living in booths they built from tree branches they gathered. They remembered how God had cared for His people in the desert for forty years while they looked for the Promised Land. It was a happy "camping out" kind of celebration. Mothers and fathers and all of their children enjoyed themselves and remembered the goodness of God.

God wanted His people to enjoy life and to trust Him. These festivals brought friends and families together to praise God and talk about what He had done for them. They were occasions everyone looked forward to, and they brought God's people closer to Him.

Discussion

Like those celebrations in the Bible, our celebration of Independence Day includes special food and activities. What are some things we do to celebrate today that they did not do in Bible times? Independence day is not a religious festival, but we can make sure to honor God on that day. How can we honor Him on July 4th?

Bible Verse

". . . proclaim liberty throughout the land. . . ." (Leviticus 25:10)

An important symbol of American freedom is the Liberty Bell. When it was formed more than two-hundred years ago, this Bible verse was engraved on it. This shows that America's founding fathers knew that liberty came from God. Many early American documents, such as the Declaration of Independence, and even buildings from early America contain Bible verses and references to God. Let us remember to thank God on July 4th for our liberty.

Independence Day

Craft: Firecracker Centerpiece

Materials

- toilet paper tube
- white or gold pipe cleaners
- gold or silver star stickers
- red, white and blue wrapping paper, any style
- star pattern below or foam star
- black felt-tip pen
- tape
- glue

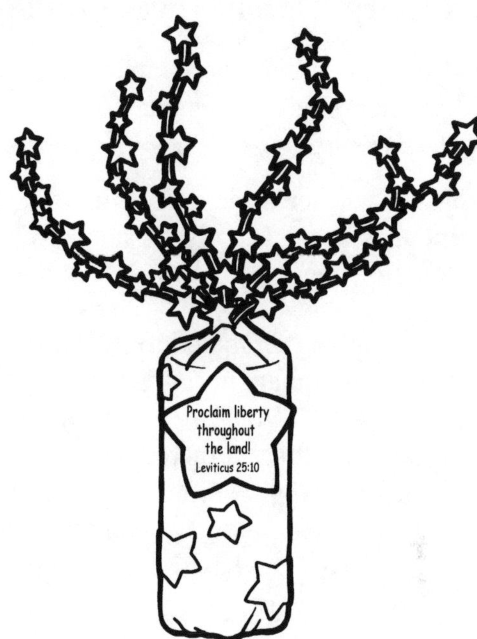

Finished Product

Directions

1. Wrap the paper tube with wrapping paper and tape to secure it. Fold the extra paper inside the tube.
2. Poke four or five pipe cleaners up through the tube. (Tape them inside the tube.)
3. Attach stickers to the pipe cleaners, several on each one.
4. Write on the star: Proclaim liberty throughout the land! Leviticus 25:10
5. Glue the star on the tube.

Variation: Use silver or gold foil star-wire in place of pipe cleaners.

Star Pattern

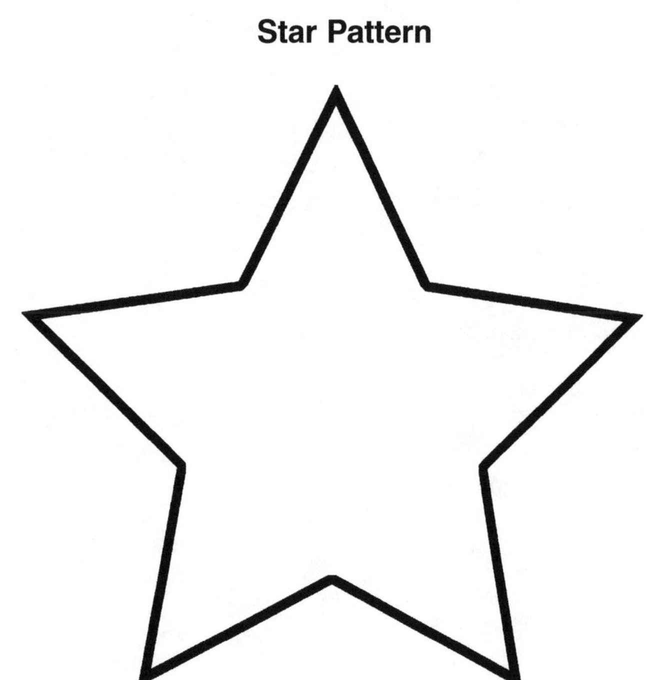

Independence Day

Bible Story: Joshua Gives People a Choice (Joshua 24:1-24)

Hand out paper and colored markers. Have each student print a sign that reads "GOD." Students should hold up their signs during the story whenever you ask a question.

Joshua was near the end of his life. He had led the Israelites through many battles against their enemies in the Promised Land. Now they were living in peace. He reminded them what God had done for them.

"Your father Abraham left his home and came to this land many years ago," Joshua said. "Who brought Abraham here?" *(Hold up "GOD" signs.)* "Then Abraham had a son, Isaac. Who gave him a son?" *(Hold up "GOD" signs.)* "Jacob and his sons went down to Egypt and their children multiplied there. Then they became slaves. Who rescued them from that land?" *(Hold up "GOD" signs.)* Your fathers and mothers wandered in the desert for many years. Who protected them and gave them food and water?" *(Hold up "GOD" signs.)* "You crossed the Jordan River and have come into the Promise Land. Who brought you safely here?" *(Hold up "GOD" signs.)*

Then Joshua challenged the people, "Fear the Lord and serve Him with all faithfulness. But if serving the Lord seems undesirable to you, then choose for yourselves this day whom you will serve. Whom will you serve?" *(Hold up "GOD" signs.)*

"We will serve the Lord because He is our God!" the people said. "We will serve the Lord our God and obey Him." Then Joshua set a large stone under an oak tree as a reminder that the people had promised to serve God there on that day.

Discussion

The United States is usually called a "Christian nation." Does that mean all Americans are Christians? What does it mean? All Americans have the same choice the Israelites had—they can choose to serve God or not. Why is serving God the best choice? How can you show your thanks to God on July 4th for blessing this nation? For what would you like to thank Him?

Bible Verse

"Blessed is the nation whose God is the Lord." (Psalm 33:12a)

Though the psalm writer was not writing about the United States when he wrote this verse, it certainly sounds like America, doesn't it? How has God blessed this nation? Sing "God Bless America." (Have students hold up their "GOD" signs as they sing.)

Independence Day

Craft: Patriotic Hat

Finished Product

Materials

- patterns on pages 75 and 76
- stapler or tape
- glue
- white cardstock
- markers
- scissors

Directions

1. Copy the patterns on white cardstock. Color and cut out the patterns.
2. Glue the star and band to the hat.
3. Cut two-inch strips of cardstock paper to form a circle around each child's head. Staple the bands and attach the top hat to the front of the band with a stapler or tape.

Variation: Have children use red and blue glitter on their hats.

Star Pattern

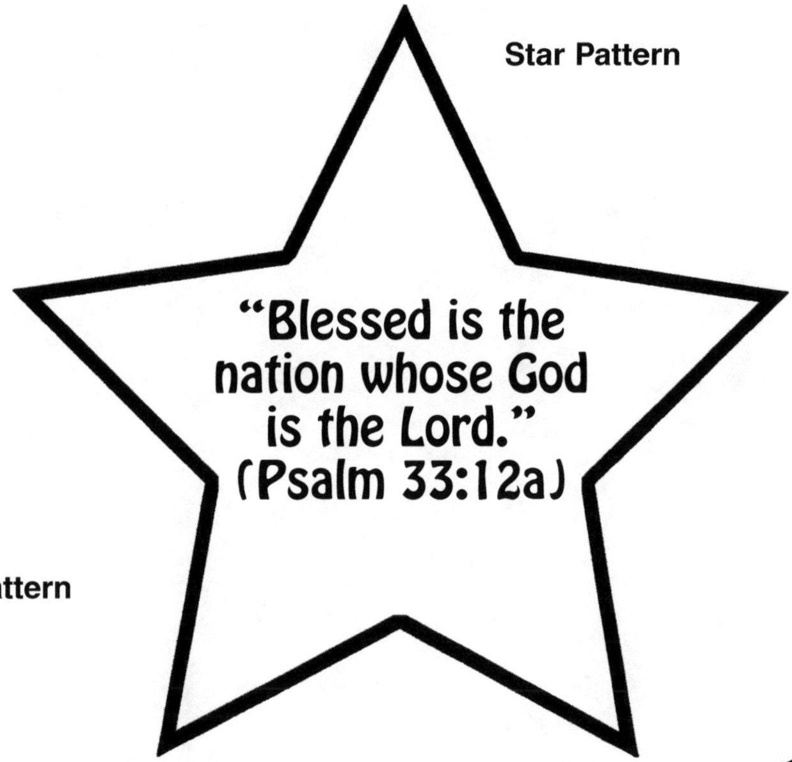

"Blessed is the nation whose God is the Lord." (Psalm 33:12a)

Hat Band Pattern

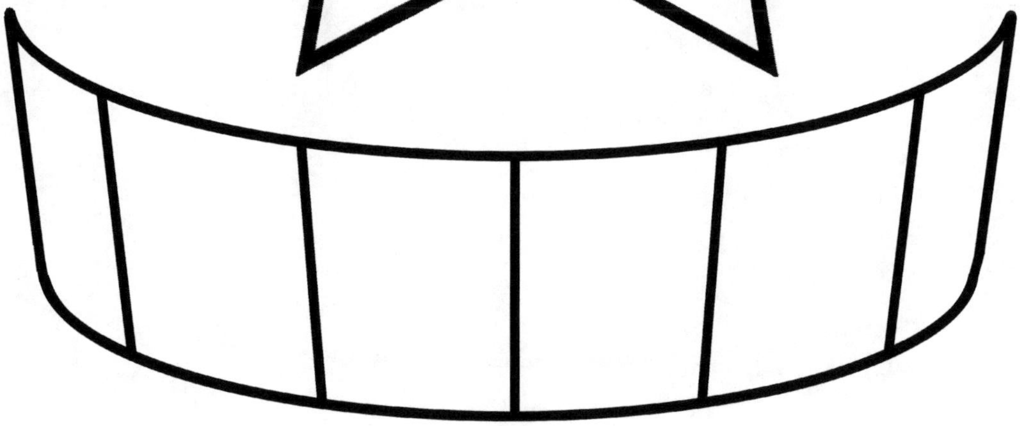

Craft: Patriotic Hat *(cont.)*

Hat Pattern

Celebrate the USA!

Independence Day

Craft: Pinwheel Pencil Topper

Materials

- two copies of the pattern below
- hole punch
- 1 1/2" straight pin with large head
- pencil
- scissors

Finished Product

Directions

1. Copy and cut out two of the patterns.
2. Cut along the four curved lines.
3. Punch holes through the circles.
4. Line up holes with middle hole.
5. Line up the two copies and poke a straight pin through.
6. Push the end of the pin into a pencil eraser.

Pinwheel Pattern

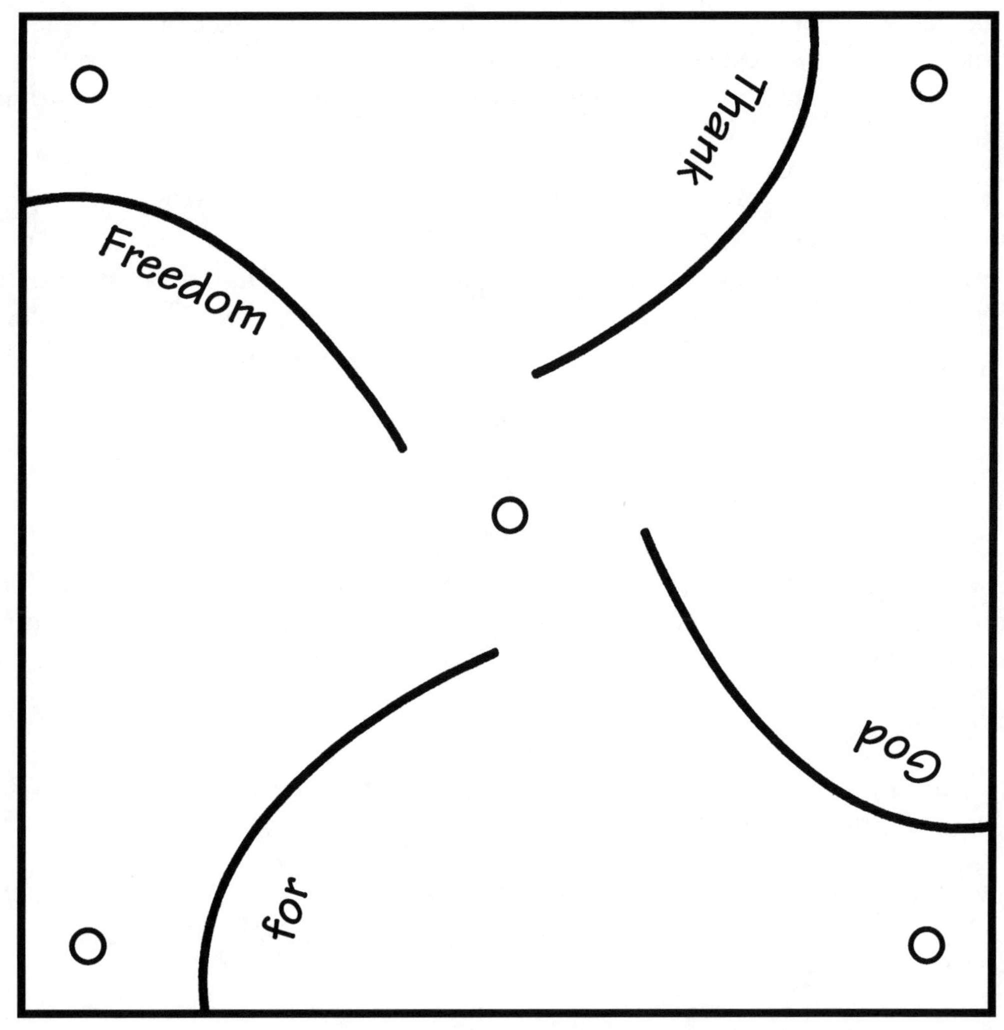

Grandparents' Day

Bible Story: Jacob Blesses His Grandsons (Genesis 48)

Tell this story from Joseph's viewpoint. You may even want to dress in an Egyptian-looking robe to make it more realistic.

> I was brought to Egypt when I was a teenager. Life was hard, but God blessed me and Pharaoh appointed me his second-in-command. I got married and had two sons. After many years, my father and brothers came to live near me in Egypt. They came at my invitation. They were here for seventeen years when I heard that my father, Jacob, was dying. I took my sons to see their grandfather one last time. Father was so glad to see us, he managed to sit up in his bed and talk with us even though he was very weak.
>
> When I told him I had brought my sons, he said, "Bring them to me so I may bless them." His sight was almost gone, so I brought my boys, Ephraim and Manasseh, close to their grandfather's bed.
>
> They were adults by now, but their grandfather hugged and kissed them. "I never expected to see your face again, and now God has allowed me to see your children, too," he told me. Then he laid his right hand on Ephraim's head and his left hand on Manasseh's head and blessed them. "May the God before whom my fathers Abraham and Isaac walked, the God who has been my shepherd all my life to this day, the Angel who has delivered me from all harm—may he bless these boys."
>
> Maybe Ephraim and Manasseh had not visited their grandfather as often as they should have, but it was obvious that he loved the two boys. My father was a man who loved God, and though he was far from perfect, he trusted God and wanted to serve Him. He was a godly influence on his grandsons, showing them the importance of following the Lord. I am glad he was able to come to Egypt so they could get to know him and learn to love and appreciate him as I did.

Discussion

Blessing children and grandchildren was a Jewish custom in Bible times. Some still do that, but today parents and grandparents pray for their children and grandchildren. What would you like your grandparents to pray for you?

Bible Verse

". . . young men and maidens, old men and children. Let them praise the name of the Lord, . . ."
(Psalm 148:12–13a)

How often do you visit your grandparents? What do you ask God to do for them?

Grandparents' Day

Craft: Bookmarks

Materials

- cardstock
- patterns on page 79 and 80
- yarn or ribbon
- scissors
- crayons or markers

Directions

1. Copy the patterns on cardstock, and choose a bookmark to color and cut out.
2. Tie yarn in the hole.
3. Give the bookmark to grandparents.

Bookmark Patterns

Young men and maidens,
old men and children.
Let them praise
the name of the Lord!
(Psalm 148:12–13a)

Craft: Bookmarks *(cont.)*

Bookmark Patterns

Gift from God
Real Friends
Accepting
Nice
Do Fun Things
Patient
Always Loving
Ready to Help
Easy to Please
Never Grouchy
Tell Stories
Special

"I always thank my God as I remember you in my prayers."

(Philemon 4)

Grandparents' Day

Bible Story: Timothy's Grandmother (2 Timothy 1:1-5; 3:14-15)

Say the story rap for students; then invite them to say it with you.

Paul had a friend named Timothy,
Two letters in the Bible are to him, you see.
Paul called him his son and he said, "I pray
For you always, every single day!"
From where did Timothy's faith come?
He was taught to love God by his mom and grandmom!
His grandmother taught his mother and then
His godly mother taught God's truth to him.
From the time he was just a baby boy,
He was learning God's Word with hope and joy.
His grandmother's faith came first, it's true,
Then she told her daughter what to do.
Then Timothy's mom showed him the way,
It was a faith chain reaction, you might say!

Discussion

Do your grandparents talk to you about the Lord? Do they encourage you to love Jesus? Have you told them what Jesus has done for you?

Bible Verse

"I always thank my God as I remember you in my prayers." (Philemon 4)

How often do you pray for your grandparents? What do you ask God for them?

Craft: Flowerpot Photo Card

Materials

- patterns on pages 82 and 83
- crayons or markers
- cardstock
- picture
- scissors
- tape

Directions

1. Copy page 82 on cardstock.
2. Flip the paper over. Copy page 83 on the other side. Fold the footer under before copying page 83.
3. Fold in half. The flowerpot with the photo should be the front of the card. (See illustration.)
4. Cut out the center of the front of the card. Tape your picture inside.
5. Give the card to grandparents.

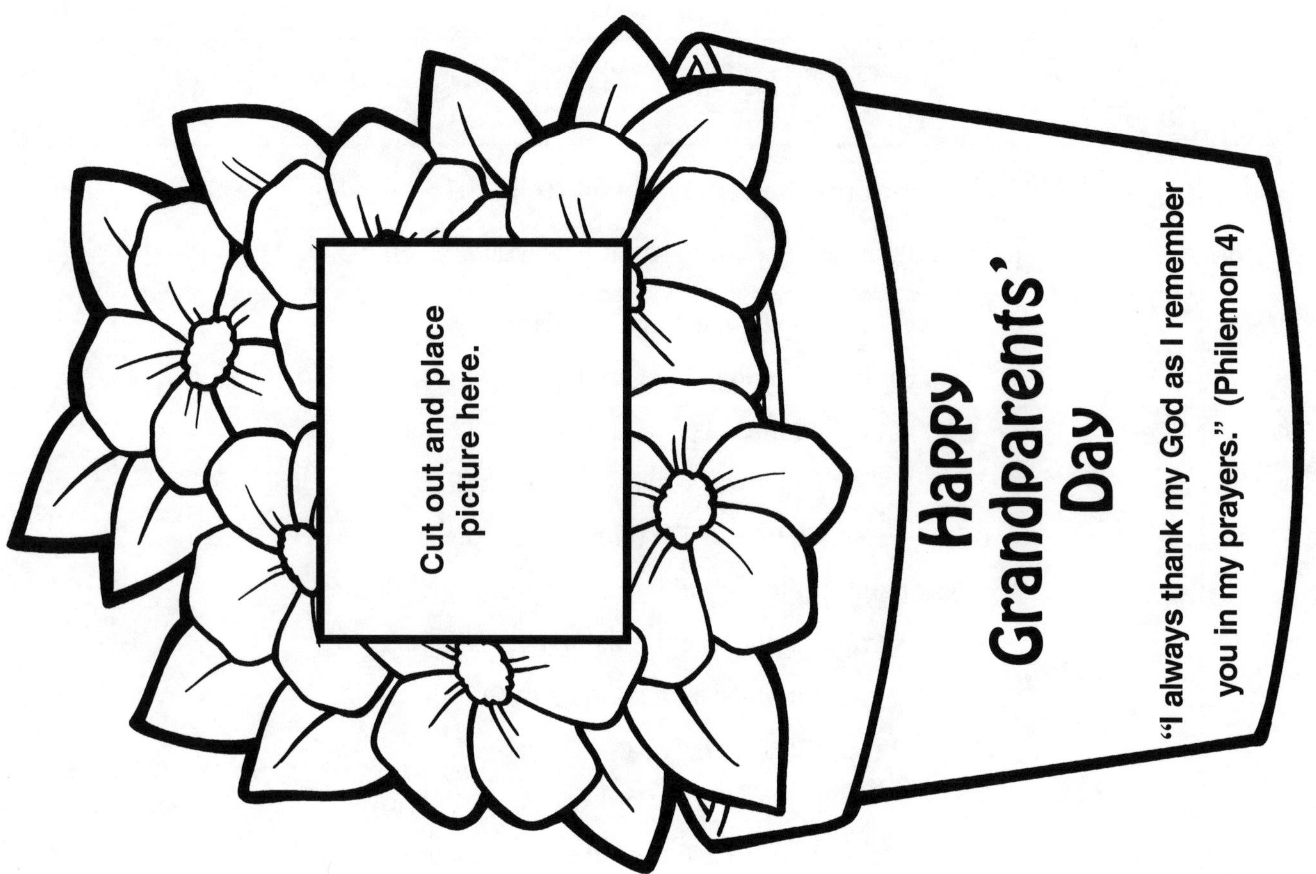
Cut out and place
picture here.
Happy
Grandparents'
Day
"I always thank my God as I remember
you in my prayers." (Philemon 4)

Happy
Grandparents'
Day

When I thank God
for all the blessings,
you are at the top
of the list!

Grandparents' Day

Craft: Spoonful of Kisses

Materials

- plastic spoon
- two chocolate drop candies
- ribbon
- hole punch
- fabric 6" x 6"
- label below
- scissors

Directions

1. Place two chocolate drop candies in the spoon.
2. Wrap the fabric over and around the spoon.
3. Tie the fabric together with ribbon.
4. Cut out the label and sign your name on it.
5. Punch out the hole.
6. Attach the label to the ribbon.

Finished Product

Label

Thanksgiving Day

Bible Story: Abraham and Sarah Have a Son (Genesis 18:1-15; 21:1-7)

Have students turn to Genesis in their Bibles. As you tell the story, ask questions for them to answer. Give them time to look up the verses for the answers.

Abraham and Sarah wanted children, but they were too old to have them. Years before, God had promised Abraham that He would make a great nation of his family. But how could that happen if he didn't even have a son? One day three angels visited Abraham and told him that the next year Sarah would give birth to a son. Sarah heard them and laughed at such a foolish idea. The Lord said to Abraham, "Why did Sarah laugh? Is anything too hard for the Lord?"

How old were Sarah and Abraham? Read Genesis 17:17 to find out. *(Sarah was ninety; Abraham was a hundred years old.)* Have you ever heard of anyone that old having a baby? But sure enough, at the age of ninety, she had her first child! What did they name the boy? Read Genesis 21:3 to find out. *(Isaac)* "Isaac" means *he laughs.* Sarah had laughed at the idea of having a baby in her old age, and now she was laughing with joy because God had made it happen!

Abraham and Sarah were very thankful to God for their son Isaac. They loved him very much and couldn't imagine what they would have done without him. When he grew up and wanted to get married, Abraham made sure Isaac found a good wife from among his own people rather than a girl from the ungodly people who lived around them. What was the name of the woman who married Isaac? Read Genesis 24:67 to find out. *(Rebekah)* Isaac was thankful for his godly parents who raised him to love God. When Isaac got married, he and his wife Rebekah had two sons. What were their sons' names? Read Genesis 25:25–26 to find out. *(Jacob and Esau)* Isaac taught his sons to love God.

God kept His promise to Abraham and made a great nation, the Jewish nation, from his son and grandchildren and great grandchildren. God blessed his family in a special way. God gives us parents and brothers and sisters to love and to care for us. He wants to bless our families, too.

Discussion

Why do you think God chose to bless Abraham's family in this special way? What are some ways God has blessed your family?

Bible Verse

". . . give thanks to him and praise his name." (Psalm 100:4b)

How can you show your thanks to God for your family? How can you show your thanks to your family for their love and encouragement?

Thanksgiving Day

Craft: Pumpkin Picture Frame

Materials

- pattern below and patterns on page 50
- orange and green crayons or markers
- tape
- cardstock
- family photo
- scissors

Directions

1. Copy the patterns on cardstock and cut them out. Color the pumpkin pattern.
2. Cut out the center of the pumpkin and tape a family photo in place.
3. Use the A-Frame stand, page 50, to hold the frame.

Variation: For the pumpkin pattern, use orange and green craft foam instead of cardstock.

Pumpkin Frame Pattern

Thank God for Our Family!

"Give thanks to him and praise his name."

(Psalm 100:4b)

Thanksgiving Day

Bible Story: Jesus Gives Thanks (Matthew 14:13-21; 26:26-29; John 11:38-44)

Have students fold their hands and bow their heads every time they hear the word *thanks* in the story.

We all know the Bible teaches us to give thanks (*fold hands and bow heads*) to God, but did you know that Jesus made a practice of giving thanks (*fold hands and bow heads*) to God in public? Though we do not know what He did in private, it's almost for sure that He also included thanks to God (*fold hands and bow heads*) in His personal prayers. Remember when Jesus fed five-thousand people with just five small loaves of bread and two fish? Jesus had all the people sit on the ground around Him. He gave thanks to God (*fold hands and bow heads*) for the bread; then, He broke the loaves and gave the bread and fish to the disciples. What started out as a little boy's lunch became enough to feed five-thousand people, with twelve baskets of food left over. That is more than Jesus started with!

Before His arrest and crucifixion, Jesus shared a last supper with his disciples. He took some bread, gave thanks (*fold hands and bow heads*), then broke it and passed it around for His disciples to eat. He told them that the bread represented His body which would soon be broken for them. Then He held a cup of grape juice and gave thanks (*fold hands and bow heads*) for it. As he passed the cup around and His disciples drank from it, He explained that the juice represented His blood which He would soon shed for them. Today, Christians still remember Jesus' death by sharing bread and juice in this way.

One day Jesus was called to a sick friend's home. By the time He got there, Lazarus was dead. Jesus stood outside his tomb and told people to take the stone away from the door. Then Jesus looked toward heaven and gave thanks (*fold hands and bow heads*). "Father," He prayed, "I thank you that you have heard me. I knew that you always hear me, but I said this for the benefit of the people standing here, that they may believe that you sent me." Lazarus walked out of his tomb, alive again! Jesus' thanks (*fold hands and bow heads*) to God was a testimony of His faith. We should follow His example and not be ashamed to offer God our thanks (*fold hands and bow heads*), no matter where we are.

Discussion

Is one day a year, Thanksgiving, enough time to thank God for all He does for us? How often should we thank Him? What five things do you want to thank God for today?

Bible Verse

"Give thanks to the Lord, call on his name; make known among the nations what he has done." (Psalm 105:1)

What three things are we told to do in this verse? What does it mean to "call on his name"? How can we "make known what he has done"?

Thanksgiving Day

Craft: Indian Corn Door Hanger

Materials

- patterns on pages 88 and 89
- brown yarn or jute string
- fabric in autumn colors
- scissors
- cardstock
- crayons or markers
- tape

Directions

1. Copy the three corn patterns on cardstock.
2. Color the corn to look like Indian corn.
3. Cut a 30" piece of yarn or jute. At the top, make a loop wide enough for a doorknob and tie it off for a hanger.
4. Cut out the the Indian corn and tape them together and to the yarn or jute.
5. At the top of each bunch of corn, add a piece of fabric tied in a bow.

Finished Product

Corn Pattern

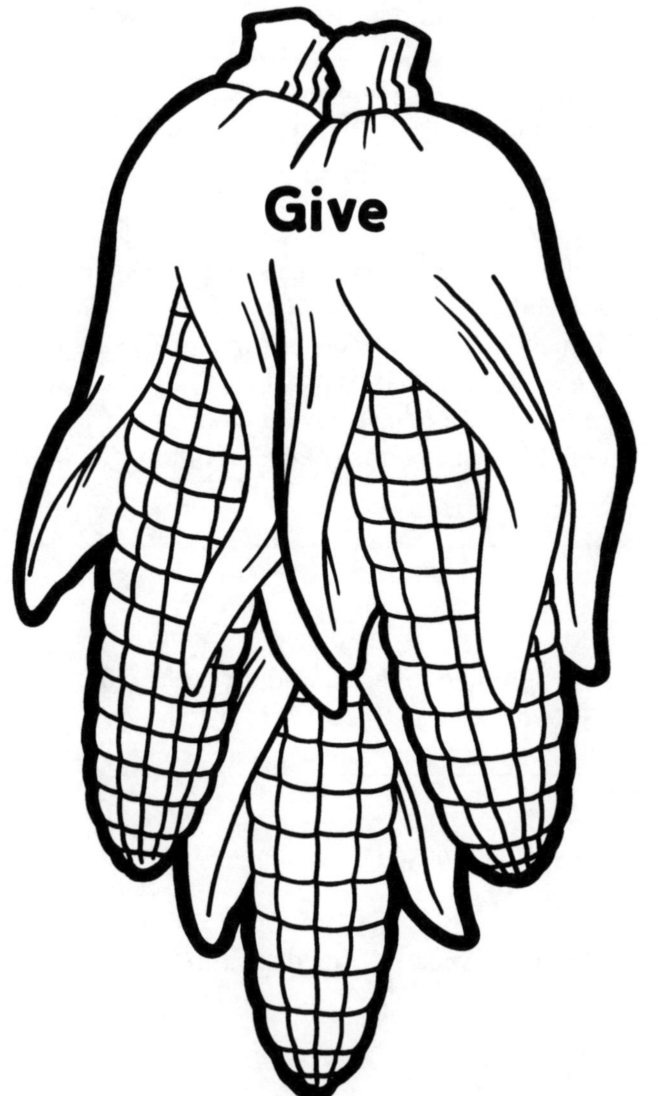

Corn Patterns

God

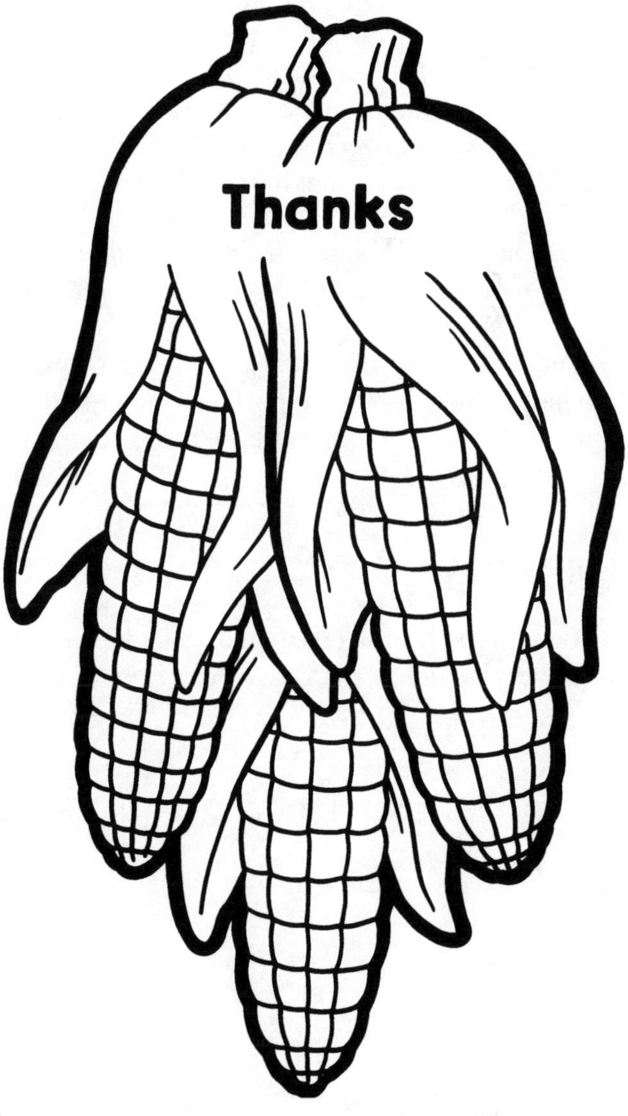

Thanks

Thanksgiving Day

Bible Story: Daniel and the Lions (Daniel 6)

Since this is such a familiar story to most children, let them help you tell it by answering questions.

Daniel was an important official in King Darius' kingdom. The king liked him so well, he planned to promote him over his other officials. They immediately became jealous and planned how they could get rid of Daniel. Of course, they could not find any way to get him into trouble because Daniel was a righteous man who led a good life. Instead, they convinced the king to make a new law that no one in the kingdom could pray to anyone except him for thirty days. Why did they think this would be a problem for Daniel? *(Daniel prayed three times a day on his knees where everyone could see him.)*

Daniel refused to stop praying because of the new law. He went home, kneeled down and gave thanks to God just as he had always done. The jealous officials reported his actions to the king and reminded him that under the new law, Daniel would have to be punished. What was the punishment? *(Daniel would be thrown into a den of lions.)* Though he did not want to do it, King Darius had Daniel thrown into the lions' den, and a stone was placed over the door.

The king could not sleep that night; he was worried about what might be happening to Daniel. Early the next morning he hurried to the lions' den and had the stone removed. What did he find? *(Daniel was unharmed.)* Daniel told the king, "My God sent his angel, and he shut the mouths of the lions. They have not hurt me because I was found innocent in His sight."

King Darius was relieved to see that God had protected Daniel. He ordered him lifted out of the den. What did the king do with the wicked officials who had tricked him into making that stupid law? *(They were thrown into the den of lions.)* God did not keep the lions from killing them. Then the king issued a decree that everyone in his kingdom should fear and respect Daniel's God. Daniel's habit of praying his thanks to God three times a day may have gotten him into trouble, but God protected him and even made an ungodly king recognize God's greatness!

Discussion

Do you think Daniel thanked God while he was in the lions' den? For what? Do you thank God for protecting you and taking care of you every day? What else has God done for you?

Bible Verse

"Give thanks to the Lord, for he is good; his love endures forever." (Psalm 107:1)

Daniel thanked God three times a day. How often do you think you should thank Him?

Thanksgiving Day

Craft: Napkin Rings and Placemat

Finished Product

Materials

- patterns on pages 91–93
- glue or tape
- crayons or markers
- cardstock
- scissors

Directions

1. Copy the patterns on cardstock. You may want to enlarge the placemat pattern. Have children color the placemat on page 93. Use clear contact paper to cover the placemat for durability or laminate it.
2. Cut out the strips on page 92 and form four circles, taping the ends to make napkin rings.
3. Color the art pieces below and cut out. Tape or glue one to each of the paper rings.
4. Place a napkin in each ring to use for Thanksgiving dinner.

Variation: Use toilet paper tubes cut into two-inch sections and paint.

Art Pieces for Napkin Rings

Craft: Napkin Rings and Placemat *(cont.)*

Paper Napkin Rings

Thank God for Our Family!

Thank God for Our Family!

Thank God for Our Family!

Thank God for Our Family!

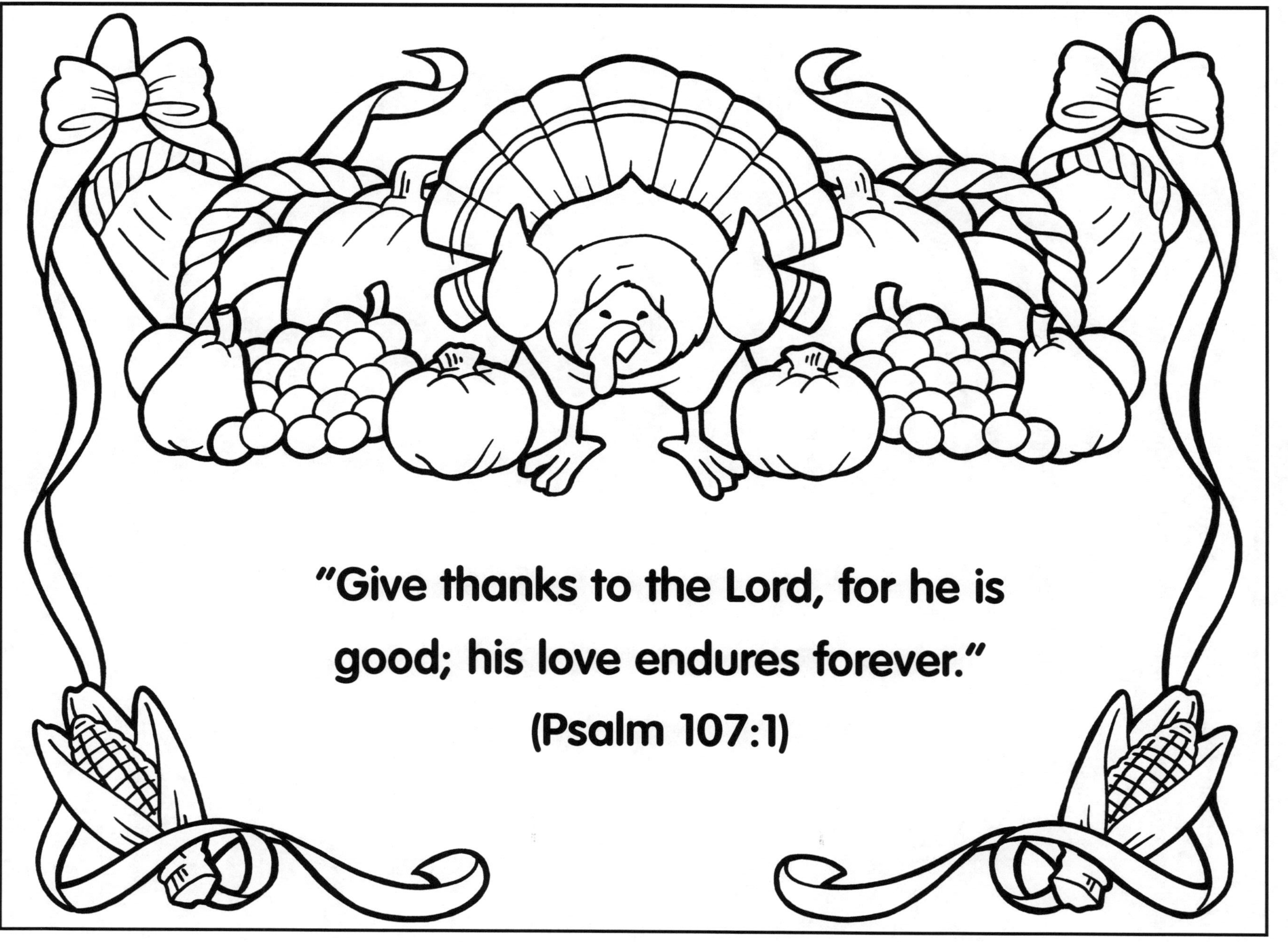
"Give thanks to the Lord, for he is
good; his love endures forever."
(Psalm 107:1)

Advent

Bible Story: An Angel Visits Mary (Luke 1:26-38)

Sing the story song for students; then invite them to sing it with you.

(*Tune:* "When Johnny Comes Marching Home Again")

God sent the angel Gabriel to earth one day
To visit a girl in Nazareth and then to say,
"Don't be afraid, God's chosen you, and I will tell you what to do
For you're highly favored and the Lord's with you."

Mary, you will have a baby boy, God's Son.
He will be great, and He will be the holy One.
Listen to me carefully, name Him Jesus for He'll be
The Messiah-Savior come to set us free.

Mary said, "How can this be? What shall I do?"
The angel said, "The Spirit will come over you.
Jesus will be God's own Son. Today salvation has begun.
For nothing is impossible with God."

Discussion

Jesus means "Savior." Why was that a good name for Him? What would Jesus do for people? How?

Bible Verse

"You will be with child and give birth to a son, and you are to give him the name Jesus." (Luke 1:31)

The person God chose to be the mother of His only Son was just a young girl. Why do you think He chose Mary? (*Hint:* Read Luke 1:46–55.)

Advent

Craft: Advent Calendar

Materials

- cardstock
- crayons or markers
- sharp cutting knife (adult use only)

Directions

1. Copy the patterns on pages 96 and 97 on cardstock.
2. Color the pictures.
3. Have an adult use a sharp knife to cut out the numbered doors on the dashed lines. Cut only three sides, leave the top attached.
4. Attach page 96 behind page 97. Make sure to line up the calendar.
5. Flip up a number each day to reveal what is under it.

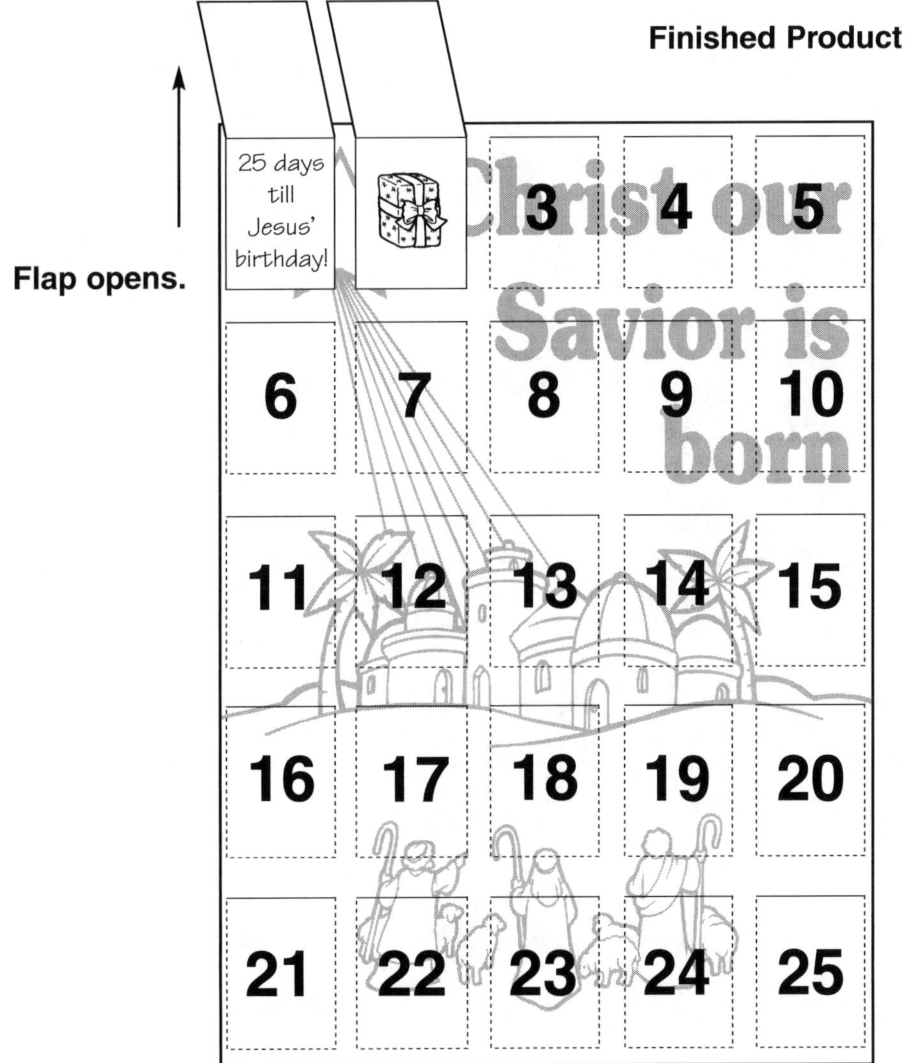

25 days till Jesus' birthday!		The virgin will give birth to a son. Isaiah 7:14	The angel said, "For nothing is impossible with God." Luke 1:37	
"I am the Lord's servant," Mary answered. Luke 1:38a	Micah said Jesus would be born in Bethlehem. Micah 5:2		An angel told Joseph, "Give Him the name Jesus." Matthew 1:21	Angels told shepherds of Jesus' birth. Luke 2:8, 11
	Jesus was born in a stable. Luke 2:7	Jesus' first bed was a manger. Luke 2:7		Angels said, "A Savior has been born to you!" Luke 2:11
Shepherds left their sheep to find Jesus. Luke 2:16		Later, wise men came looking for Jesus. Matthew 2:1–2	God led the wise men to Jesus by a special star. Matthew 2:9	
The wise men gave gifts to Jesus. Matthew 2:11	Jesus came to save people from their sins. Matthew 1:21		Jesus is the way, the truth, and the life—the only way to God! John 14:6	**Happy Birthday, Jesus!**

Christ our Savior is born

1	2	3	4	5
6	7	8	9	10
11	12	13	14	15
16	17	18	19	20
21	22	23	24	25

Advent

Bible Story: An Angel Visits Joseph (Matthew 1:18-25)

Choose a good reader to read the part of Joseph. You read the part of the interviewer. To make the interview more realistic, use a microphone (real or homemade).

Interviewer:	We're at the home of Joseph the Carpenter here in Nazareth to ask him about some rumors we've been hearing. Joseph, thank you for allowing us into your home.
Joseph:	That's okay.
Interviewer:	The rumor is that you had an unusual visitor recently. Is it true?
Joseph:	Yes, an angel came to give me a message from God. He appeared to me in a dream.
Interviewer:	Why did he come?
Joseph:	Well, I'm engaged to a girl named Mary, and I just found out that she's expecting a baby.
Interviewer:	Wait a minute! You're not going to go ahead and marry her, are you?
Joseph:	Of course. I had thought of quietly calling it off, but that was before the angel spoke to me. He told me not to be afraid to marry her because the baby in her womb was conceived by the Holy Spirit. It is a miracle baby, God's own Son.
Interviewer:	You mean, the Messiah we've been hearing about for so many years?
Joseph:	That's right; that was God's message for me. I know it sounds crazy, but I believe God. The angel said I'm to name the baby Jesus because He will save His people from their sins.
Interviewer:	So you've talked with Mary and told her about seeing this angel?
Joseph:	Certainly, but she wasn't that surprised. An angel came to her sometime ago to tell her she would give birth to God's Son. Remember that verse in the book of Isaiah about the Messiah: "The virgin will be with child and will give birth to a son, and they will call him Immanuel—which means, 'God with us'"? Well, this is the fulfillment of that promise. And I am to be a part of it!
Interviewer:	Do your families and neighbors all believe your angel stories?
Joseph:	Oh no; some of them refuse to believe us. But to whom should we listen—other people or God? I'll listen to God, thank you. I am going to raise God's Son here on Earth! Wow!
Interviewer:	That's our report for today from Nazareth. Thanks for tuning in.

Discussion

What does *Immanuel* mean? Why was God sending His Son to earth as a baby?

Bible Verse

"The virgin will be with child and will give birth to a son, and they will call him Immanuel—which means, 'God with us.'" (Matthew 1:23)

How is Jesus "God with us"?

Advent

Craft: Glitter Christmas Card

"They will call him Immanuel—
which means, 'God with us.'"
(Matthew 1:23)

Finished Product

Materials

- patterns on pages 99 and 100
- green glitter
- glue
- cardstock
- aluminum foil
- scissors

Directions

1. Copy the patterns below and all of page 100 on cardstock.
2. Fold the card, page 100, in half with the design showing on the front of the card.
3. Cut out the Christmas tree pattern and smear glue over the squiggle mark.
4. Sprinkle with green glitter over the glue.
5. Cut out the star and wrap foil around it. Glue the tree to the front of the card. Glue the star on top.
6. Write a message inside and give the card to a special friend.

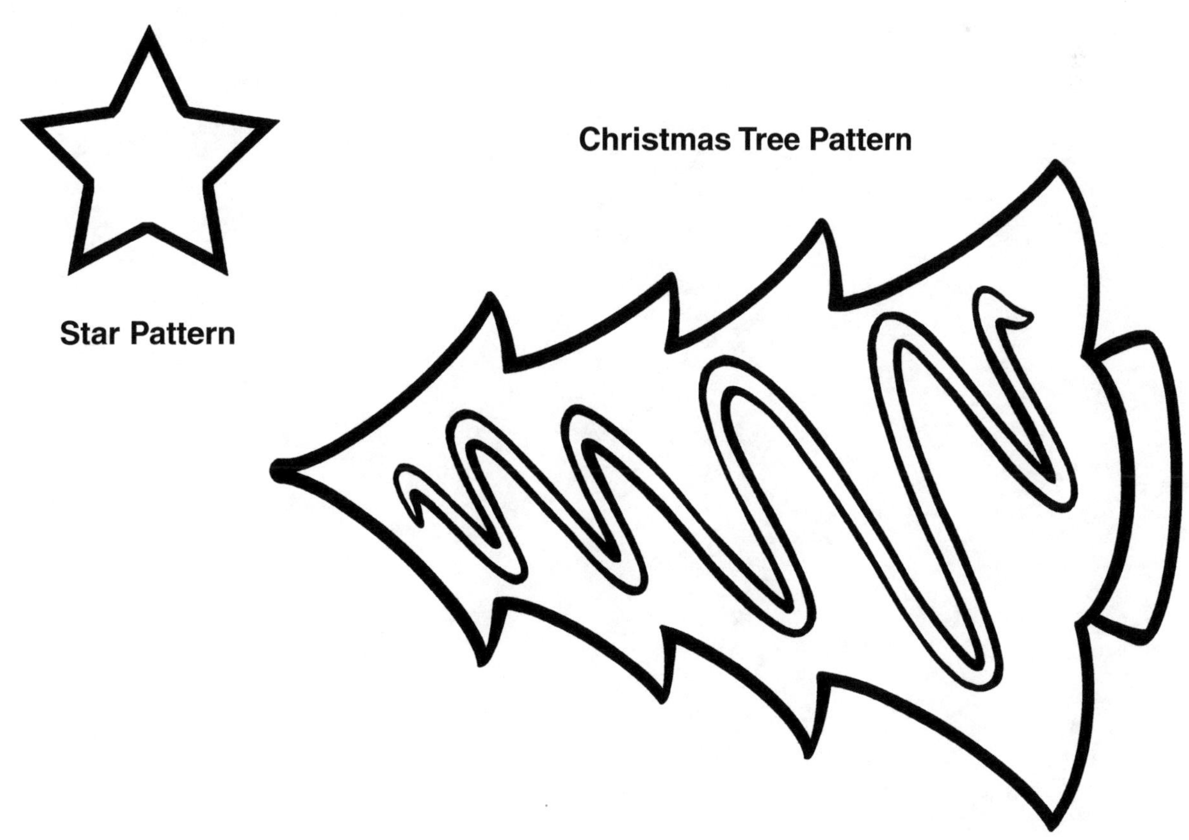

Star Pattern
Christmas Tree Pattern

"They will call him Immanuel—
which means, 'God with us.'"
(Matthew 1:23)

Christmas

Bible Story: Jesus Is Born (Luke 2:1-7)

As you tell the story, let students act it out, walking around the room from Nazareth to Bethlehem, knocking on the inn door to ask for a room, going to the stable out back, moving the animals to make a place for Mary, etc. To make the story more realistic, set up a corner of the room with some hay or shredded paper, a box for a manger, and some stuffed animals to represent the stable.

Caesar Augustus, the Roman emperor who ruled over Israel, decreed that everyone in the empire had to take part in a census so the people could all be counted. Each person had to go to his hometown to register for the census. This was not good news for Joseph. Mary, his wife, was due to have her baby any time. He could not leave her home by herself, so they went together to Bethlehem. Since they did not have much money, they probably walked the whole way, though Joseph may have borrowed a donkey for Mary on which to ride. (*Walk around the room as if going to Bethlehem.*)

When they got to Bethlehem, the town was crowded with people who had come to register for the census. The inn was full, leaving no room for them. (*Pretend to knock on a door, then turn away sadly.*) Joseph took Mary, instead, to a stable where animals were kept. It probably smelled like animals and may not have been too clean, but at least tired Mary had a place to rest. (*Have children lie down in the stable area on the floor.*) It was a good thing they found the stable when they did, because that night Mary's baby, God's Son, was born. Mary wrapped the infant in some cloths she had brought along and laid him in a manger, an animal's feeding trough. Throughout the night as she cared for her baby and rocked him in her arms, she must have looked around the stable and thought, "What a strange place for the Son of God to begin His life on Earth." (*Pretend to rock the baby in your arms.*) But the place of His birth didn't matter. Jesus had come to earth to save people from their sins!

Discussion

Why do you think God chose to have His Son be born in a stable instead of a palace? Do you think the time and place of Jesus' birth was an accident or God's plan? Why?

Bible Verse

"For God so loved the world that he gave his one and only Son, that whoever believes in him shall not perish but have eternal life." (John 3:16)

God sent His Son to Earth because He loves people, and He wants us to be in heaven with Him. What did Jesus do to make that possible? What do we need to do to have eternal life?

Christmas

Craft: Shoebox Manger Scene

Materials

- patterns on pages 102–104
- crayons or markers
- hay or straw (yellow paper slivers)
- cotton balls
- toilet paper tubes (3 or 4)
- cardstock
- shoebox
- brown paint and paintbrushes
- tape or glue
- scissors

Directions

1. Paint the shoebox brown.
2. Glue some hay or straw on the inside of the shoebox for a floor.
3. Draw a window on the shoebox.
4. Copy the patterns onto cardstock.
5. Color and cut out the patterns.
6. Glue cotton on the sheep figures.
7. Cut the paper tubes into 1" to 1 1/2" rings, one for each figure.
8. Tape or glue a tube to the back of each figure so it stands up.
9. Arrange the figures in and around the shoebox stable.

Finished Product

Baby Jesus

Mary

Craft: Shoebox Manger Scene *(cont.)*

Cow

Joseph

Sheep

Shepherd

Donkey

Craft: Shoebox Manger Scene *(cont.)*

Camel

Wise Men

Christmas

Bible Story: Wise Men Visit Jesus (Matthew 2:1-12)

As you tell the story, draw stick figures on the board to represent the wise men, King Herod, Mary, and Jesus. Hand out paper and pencils and have students draw their own stick figures to illustrate the events of the story.

> About the time Jesus was born, wise men from the east saw a special star in the sky. (*Draw a star.*) Somehow they knew that the star meant that the Messiah-King had come. They immediately left their homes and began a long trip to find the King. (*Draw three stick people.*) They were important, wealthy men and probably rode camels across the desert. They headed for Jerusalem, the capital city of Israel. Where else would they find a king? When they arrived, the wise men went to King Herod, the man in charge, to ask where the new King of the Jews could be found. (*Draw a stick figure wearing a crown.*) "We saw his star in the east and have come to worship him," they said.
>
> Herod suddenly became disturbed. Had a new king been born who would take over his job? As he thought about it, he called together all the chief priests and teachers of the law to find an answer to the wise men's question. They looked into God's Word and found that the prophet Micah had prophesied that the Messiah would be born in Bethlehem. When the wise men heard this, they turned to leave, but Herod stopped them. "When did you first see this star?" he asked them. They told him it had been about two years ago. Then he asked them to let him know when they found the baby because he wanted to go and worship him, too. (*Erase all drawings. Draw three stick figures following the star on another part of the board.*)
>
> The wise men left Jerusalem and followed the special star to the town of Bethlehem. They went to the house where Joseph's family was living. (*Draw a house.*) The wise men were overjoyed to see the Christ Child with His mother. (*Draw a stick figure for Mary and a small one for Jesus.*) They bowed down and worshiped Jesus, then offered Him wonderful gifts: (*Draw three gift-wrapped packages.*) gold, sweet smelling incense, and myrrh. Myrrh was a rather strange gift for a young child. It was an ointment most often used on dead bodies before wrapping them in cloths and burying them.
>
> The wise men headed home the next day, but decided to take a different route after an angel warned them in a dream not to return to King Herod. Their long trip had been worth it—they had seen God's king and had been able to worship Him and give Him their gifts of love.

Discussion

How do you think the wise men knew that the star meant the Messiah had been born? By the time they found Jesus, he was about two years old, and he and Mary and Joseph were no longer in the stable, but in a house. What do you think Jesus thought of the gifts the wise men gave Him? They may have been strange gifts for a two year old, but they probably came in handy when an angel later warned Joseph to take his family to Egypt to escape Herod. Joseph probably sold the gifts for money to travel and live in Egypt for awhile. Even the gifts the wise men brought Jesus were a part of God's perfect plan!

Bible Story: Wise Men Visit Jesus (Matthew 2:1-12) *(cont.)*

Bible Verse

". . . they bowed down and worshiped him. Then they opened their treasures and presented him with gifts of gold and of incense and of myrrh." (Matthew 2:11b)

Why do we give gifts to those we love at Christmas? Jesus was God's special gift to all people, but we can give Him gifts, too. What can you give Jesus? What does He want most from all of us?

Craft: Christmas Gift Bags

Materials

- patterns on pages 106 and 107
- white paper
- crayons or markers
- paper bag with handles
- scissors
- glue

Directions

1. Copy the patterns on white paper.
2. Color and cut them out.
3. Glue the patterns to the front and back of a bag.

Jesus
is the
Best Gift
of
All!

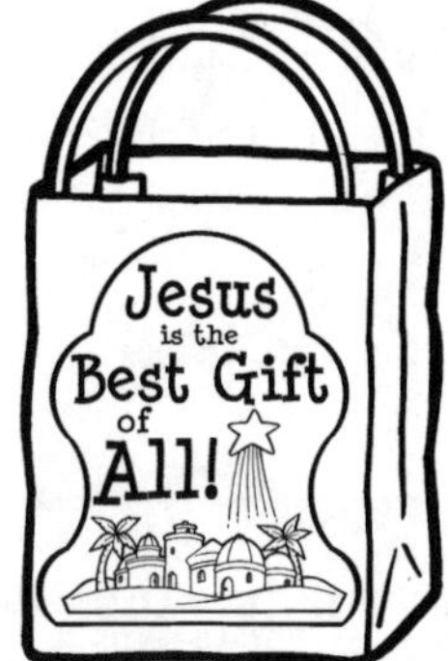

Finished Product

Christmas Gift Bag Pattern

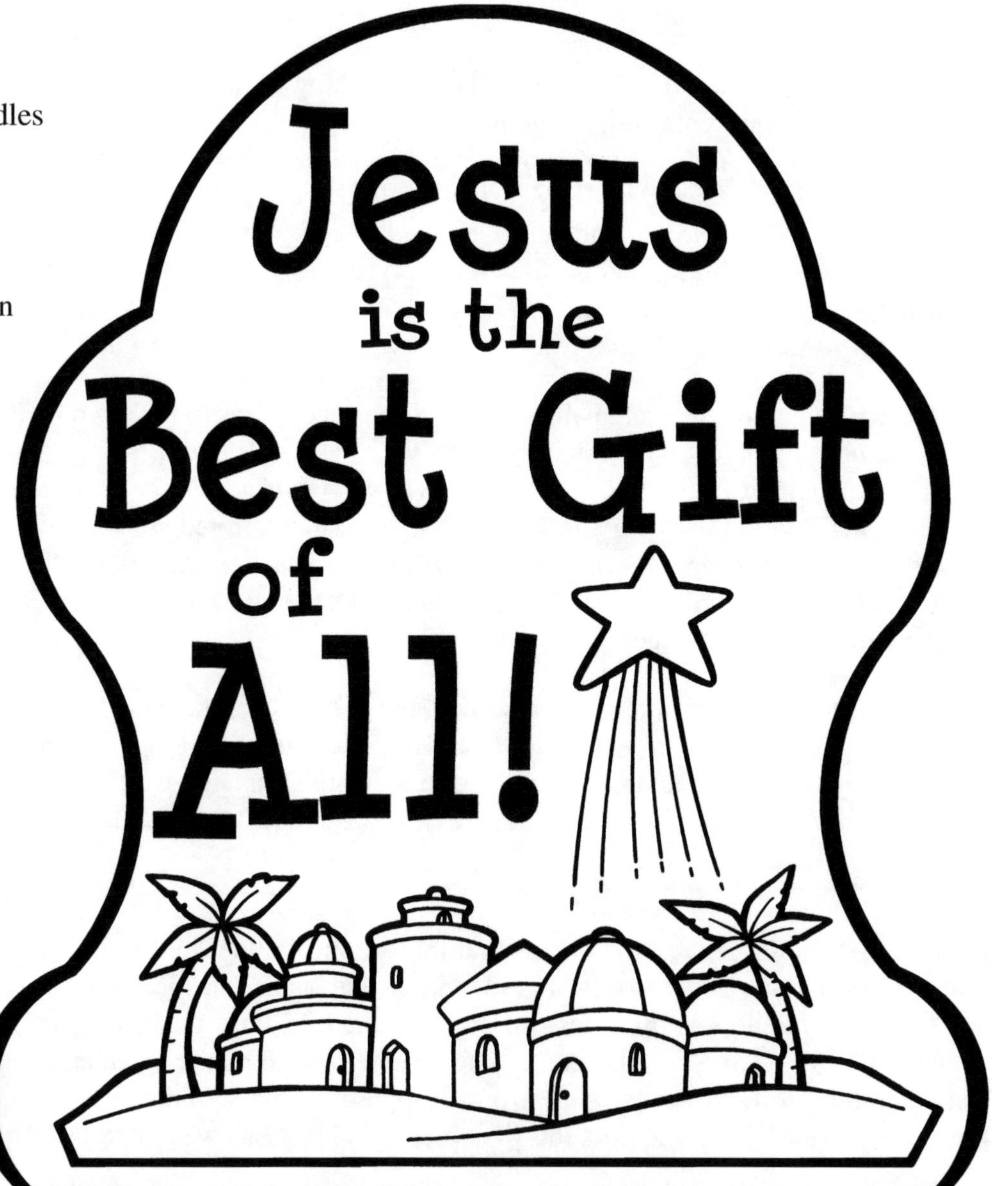

Jesus
is the
Best Gift
of
All!

Craft: Christmas Gift Bags *(cont.)*

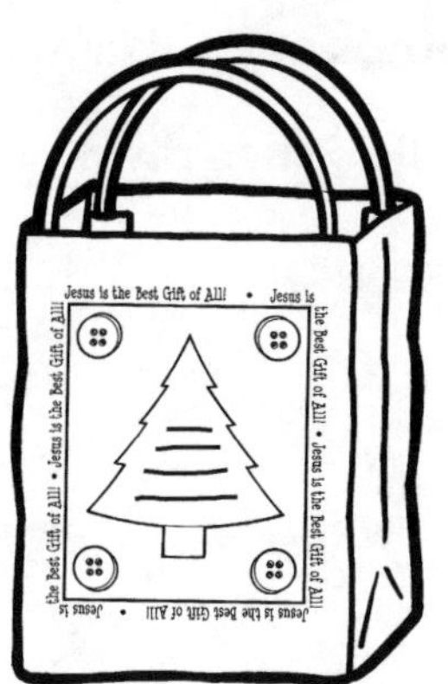

Finished Product

Christmas Gift Bag Pattern

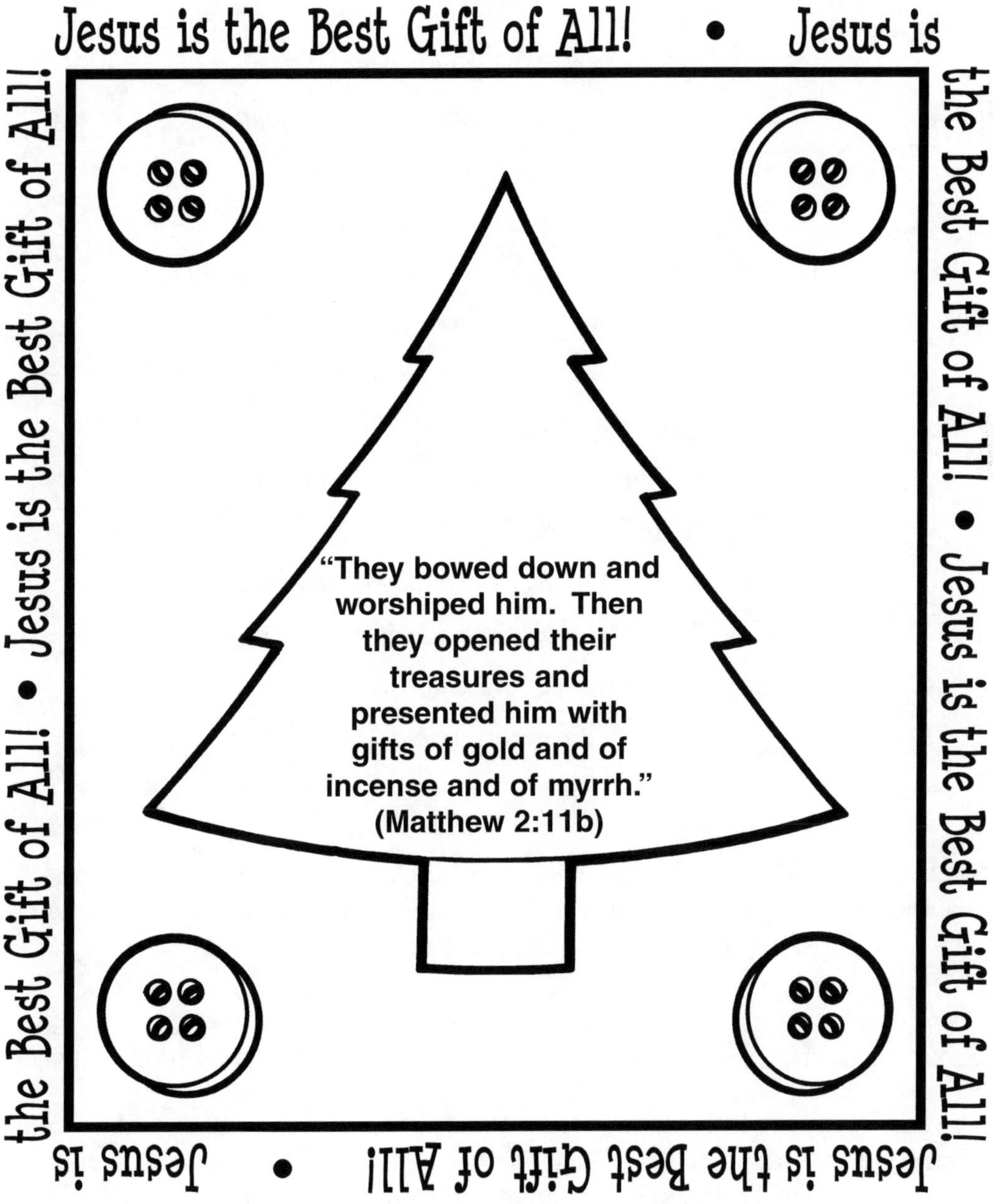

Jesus is the Best Gift of All! • Jesus is the Best Gift of All! • Jesus is the Best Gift of All! • Jesus is the Best Gift of All! • Jesus is the Best Gift of All!

"They bowed down and worshiped him. Then they opened their treasures and presented him with gifts of gold and of incense and of myrrh." (Matthew 2:11b)

Christmas

Bible Story: Angels Announce Jesus' Birth (Luke 2:8-20)

Say the action rhyme, encouraging students to clap with you, wave their hands, and do the other actions. Then let them try saying the complete rhyme with the actions.

Shepherds in the field (*Clap, clap, clap*)
Watching over their sheep. (*Baa, baa, baa!*)
Very, very tired, (*Yawn, stretch*)
Almost asleep. (*Drop head and close eyes.*)
Suddenly awake! (*Jerk head up and open eyes.*)
A big, bright light! (*Shake hands over your head.*)
Angels in the sky, (*Wave hands over your head.*)
Shattering the night! (*Clap hands and jump.*)
Joyful news—(*Clap, clap, clap*)
Christ the Lord is here! (*Hooray!*)
Lying in a manger (*Rock arms as if rocking a baby.*)
In a stable near. (*Point over your shoulder.*)
Go find the baby (*Turn around quickly and run in place.*)
In the manger bed. (*Rock arms as if rocking a baby.*)
He's the Son of God (*Kneel down.*)
As the angels said. (*While kneeling down, raise hands over head.*)
Tell everybody (*Turn quickly from one person to another.*)
Of the stable birth. (*Rock arms as if rocking a baby.*)
Praise God above (*Clap hands over your head.*)
And God on the earth! (*Clap, clap, clap*)

Discussion

Imagine you were a shepherd on the night of Jesus' birth. How would you have reacted to the angels' message? What did the shepherds do as soon as they saw Jesus for themselves? How can we do the same thing today? Is Christmas a good time to tell people about Jesus? Why?

Bible Verse

"Today in the town of David a Savior has been born to you; he is Christ the Lord." (Luke 2:11)

The angel told Mary to call her baby Jesus. He told Joseph the baby's name would be Immanuel. In this verse are three more names for Jesus. What are they? What do they mean? (*Savior*—one who saves, the same as Jesus; Christ—Messiah or Anointed One; Lord—Master)

Craft: Christmas Noel Hanging

Finished Product

Materials

- patterns below
- gold glitter
- magnet or ribbon
- crayons or markers
- white cardstock
- glue
- scissors

Directions

1. Copy patterns on white cardstock.
2. Color the solid NOEL background blue and cut it out in one piece.
3. Cut out the NOEL letters and glue them to the blue background.
4. Color and cut out the Baby Jesus and glue in the bottom of the "O."
5. Cut out the star. Cover it with glue and add gold glitter.
6. Glue a magnet to the back or attach a ribbon to hang the decoration.

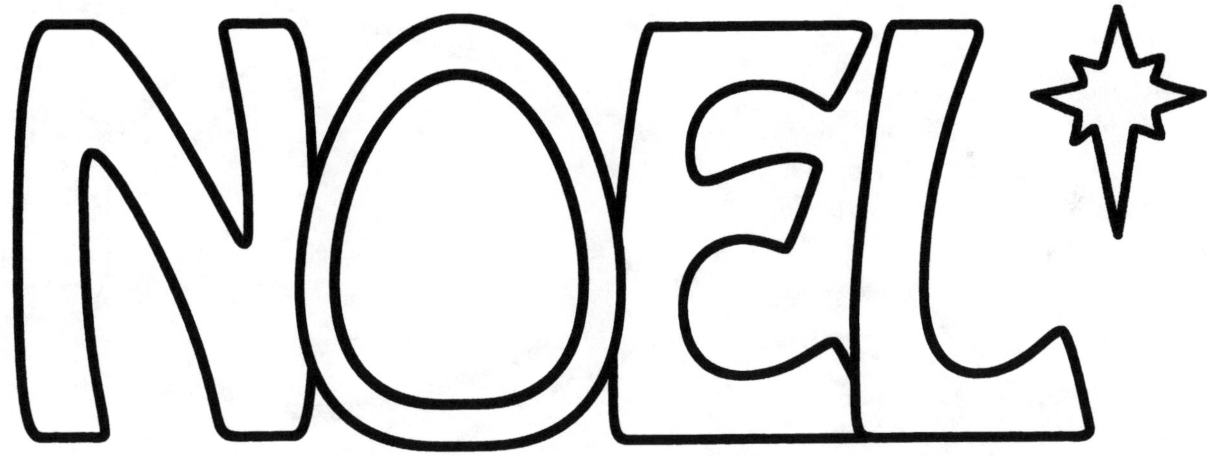

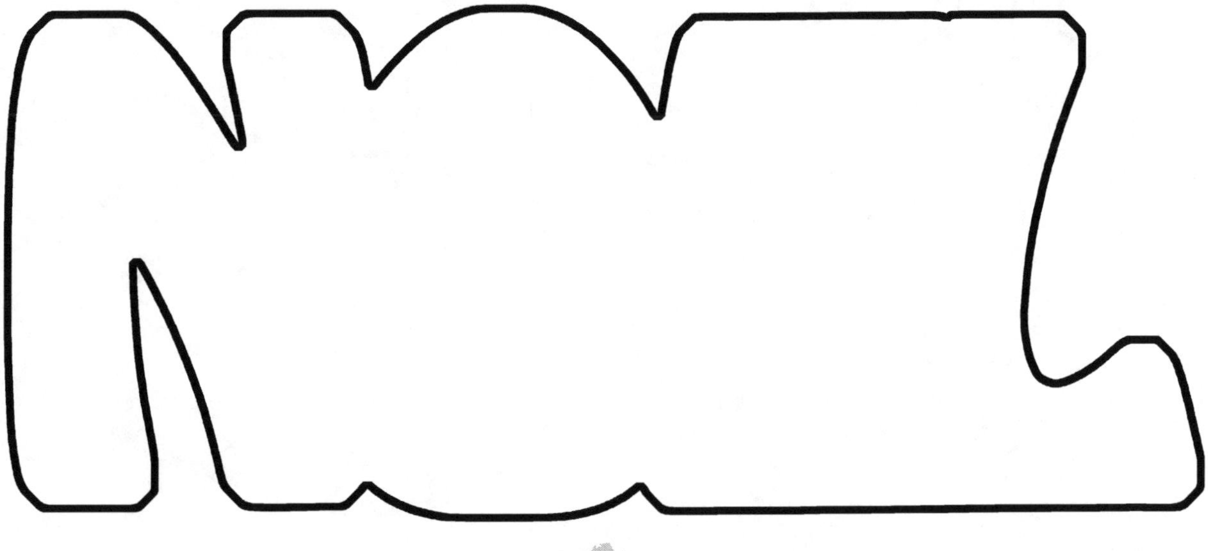

Christmas

Craft: Jesus Light Bulb Garland

Finished Product

Materials

- patterns on page 110 and 111
- cardstock
- ribbon or fabric
- tape or glue
- red yarn or jute
- scissors
- crayons or markers

Directions

1. Copy the patterns on cardstock. You will need six paper light bulbs.
2. Color and cut out the letters and bulbs.
3. Glue or tape each bulb and letter spelling out JESUS, alternating letters with light bulbs on the yarn or jute. You will need about one yard.
4. At each end, tie knots to hang the garland. Tie ribbon or fabric on each end. Hang the garland above a doorway or any special place to celebrate Jesus' birthday.

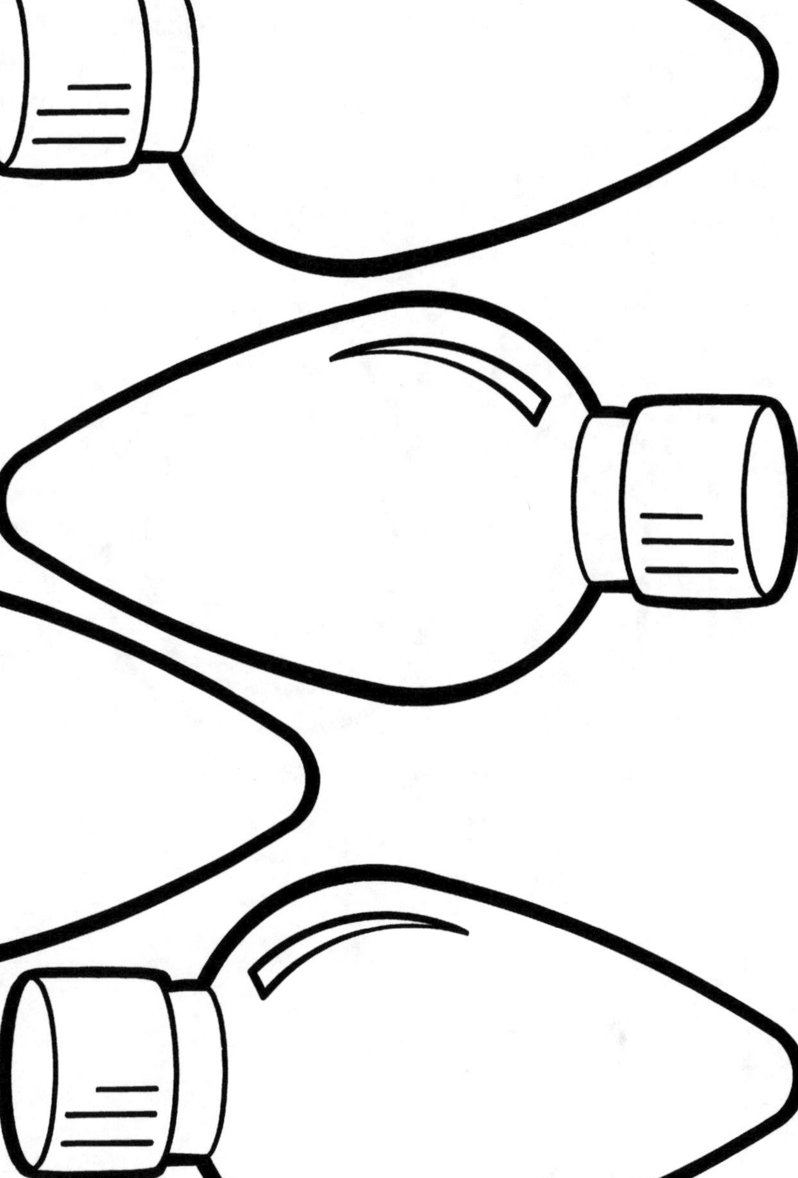

Light Bulb Patterns

Craft: Jesus Light Bulb Garland *(cont.)*

Letter Patterns

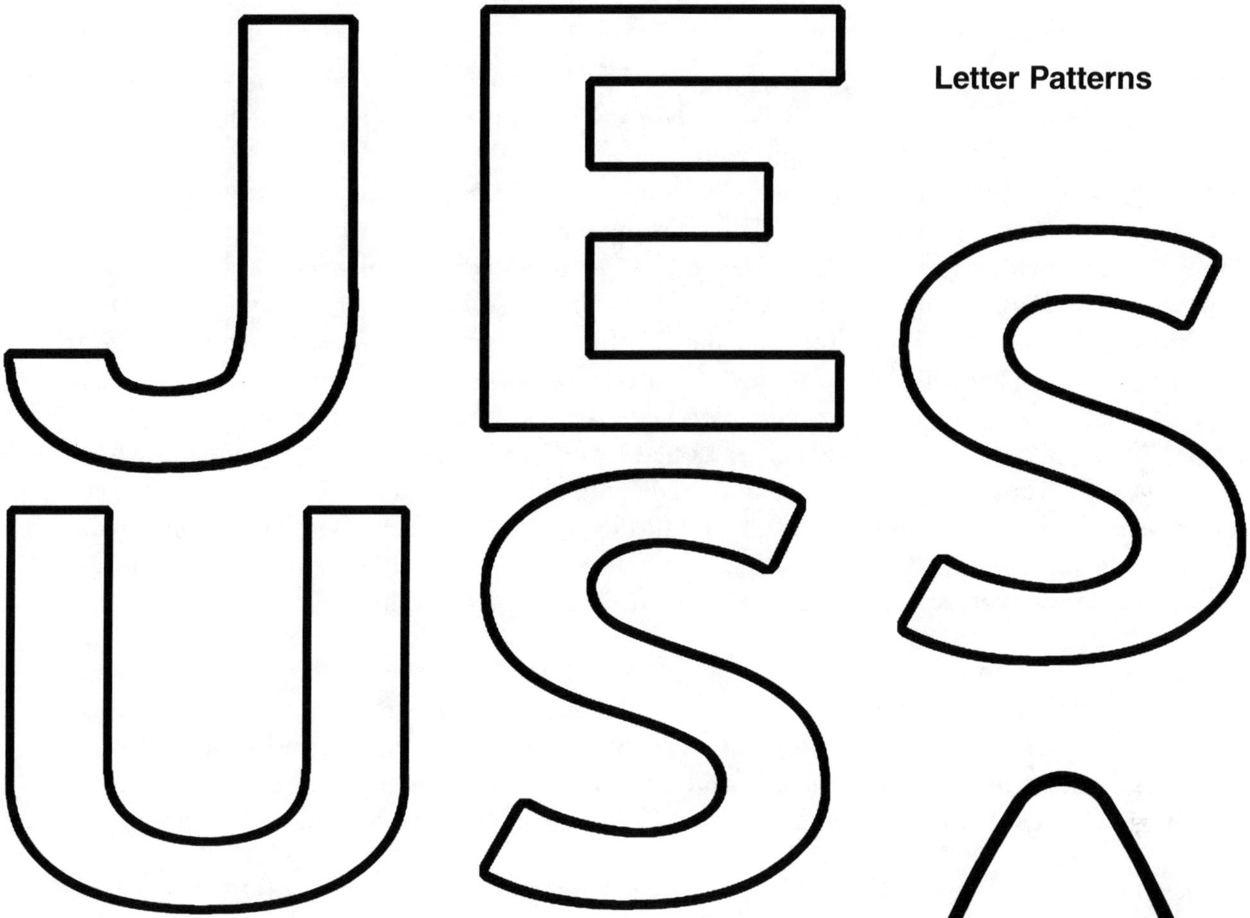

Light Bulb Patterns

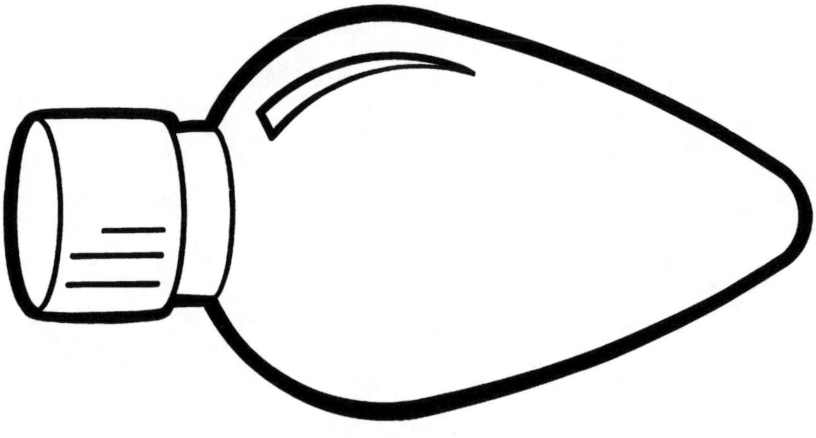

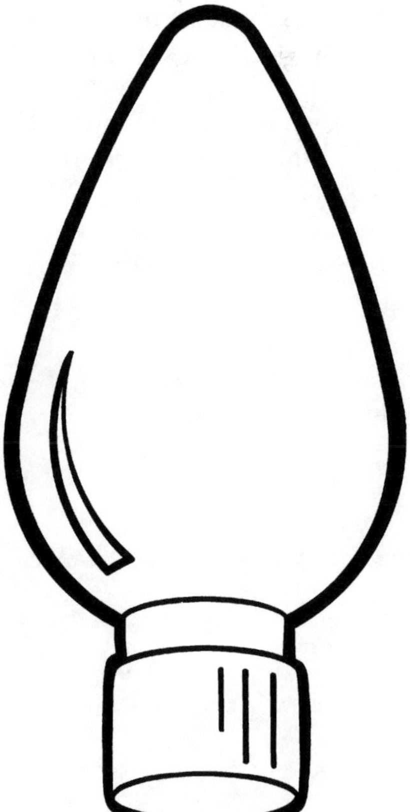

Spring

Bible Story: God Creates the World (Genesis 1; Hebrews 1:2-3)

As you tell the story, act it out and have students copy your actions.

God is the great Creator who made everything. First He made night (*Pretend to be sleeping*); then, He made day (*Yawn, stretch, and open eyes*). That was the first day of creation. On the second day He created the land (*Stomp your feet*) and the sky (*Raise your hands over your head*). Then on the third day God said, "Let the land produce seed-bearing plants and trees." Trees and bushes suddenly appeared. The trees grew tall, waving their leaves in the wind. (*Slowly sway arms over your head.*) The earth began to look beautiful with grass and trees and flowers and all kinds of plants. Then God made the sun to shine during the day (*Hold arms in circle over your head*) and the moon and stars to shine at night (*Snap hands over your head like twinkling stars*). That was the fourth day. On the fifth day God made fish and sea creatures to swim in the water (*Move hands in swimming motions*) and birds to fly in the sky (*Flap arms like wings*). The birds sang and the flowers put out a lovely fragrance and the sun shone down on the new earth. Then on the sixth day, God made animals of all kinds—kangeroos and camels, monkeys and mice, bears and bats, tigers and turtles, and much, much more. (*Pantomime some of these animals*) But God wasn't finished yet. He had one more creature to make, the best of all– man. He was very special because God made man in His own image!

God created a beautiful universe, but He did not stop there. He set everything in motion and made sure everything worked the way it should. He set the planets revolving around the huge sun so there would be seasons of different weather—spring, summer, fall, and winter. He made the earth rotate so night and day would continue. He provided rain to water the ground. And you know what God thought about everything He had made? "God saw that it was good."

In the spring, we see birds building their nests and rain and sunshine making flowers grow and trees blossom into beautiful colors. We remember that God not only made this earth, but He also sustains it. He keeps everything going according to His perfect plan.

Discussion

How did God create people to be different from animals? How can we show our appreciation for the beautiful earth God created?

Bible Verse

"You care for the land and water it; you enrich it abundantly. . . . You crown the year with your bounty, . . ." (Psalm 65:9a, 11a)

What are some ways God cares for this earth and keeps it going?

Spring

Craft: Spring Flower Mobile

Finished Product

Materials

- patterns on pages 113–115
- yellow paper
- crayons or markers
- cardstock
- string
- glue or tape
- hole punch
- scissors

Directions

1. Copy the patterns on cardstock and color them. (Make two pansy patterns. Color one yellow and one violet with black centers.) Copy several raindrops.
2. Cut out the patterns. Glue the clouds and sun together as shown.
3. Tape string of various lengths to the back of the clouds. You can also use the hole punch and tie the string.
4. To make the tulip, glue or tape the small piece to the back of the tulip pattern for a three dimensional effect. (See sample ilustration on page 115.)
5. To make the pansies, glue the one-petal piece to the back of the two-petal piece. Then glue the small circle to the top of the two-sided petals. (See sample ilustration on page 115.)
6. Punch a small circle out of yellow paper and glue to the center of the pansy.
7. Attach the flowers and raindrops to the strings hanging from the clouds.
8. Attach string to the top of the clouds and hang the mobile.

Raindrop Patterns

Craft: Spring Flower Mobile *(cont.)*

Cloud Patterns

"You care for the land and water it; you enrich it abundantly. . . . You crown the year with your bounty, . . ." (Psalm 65:9a, 11a)

Sun Pattern

Craft: Spring Flower Mobile *(cont.)*

Pansy Patterns

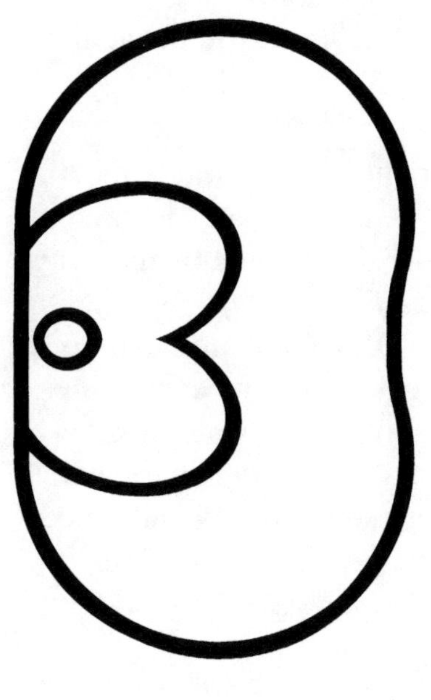

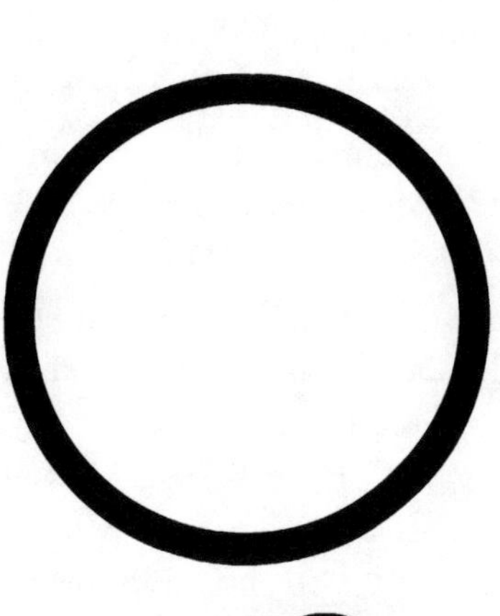

Finished Pansy

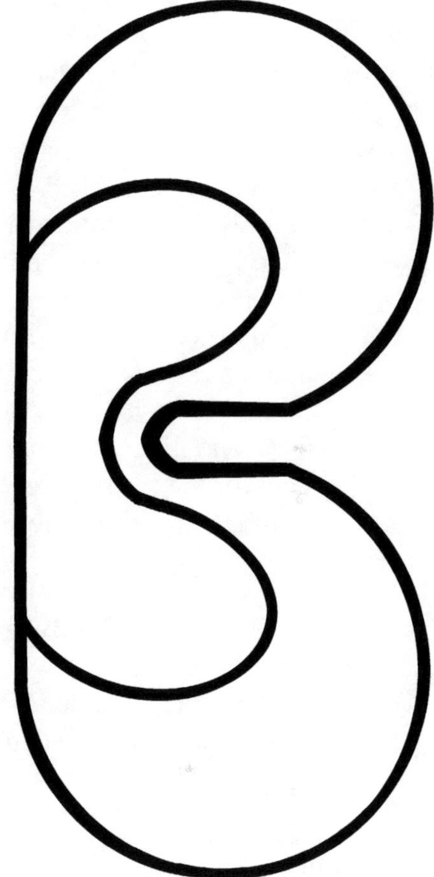

Finished Tulip

Tulip Patterns

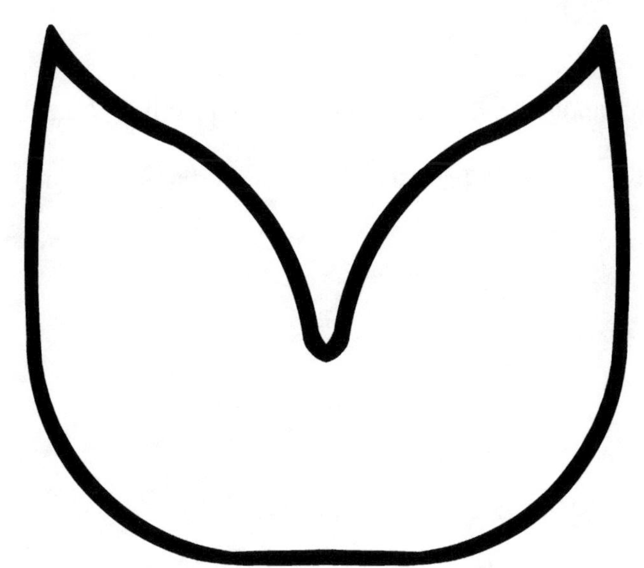

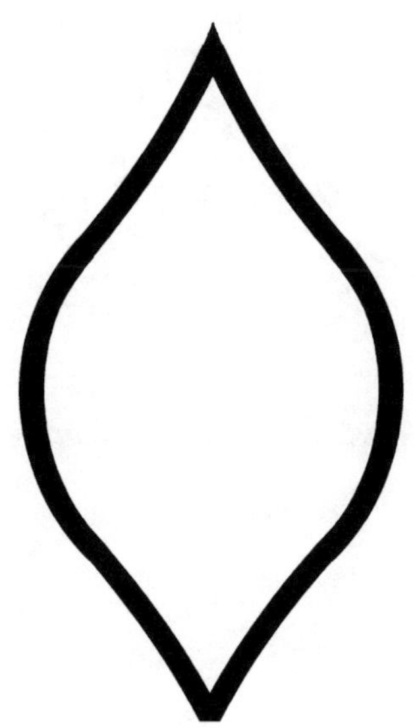

Spring

Bible Story: The Good Samaritan (Luke 10:30-37)

Choose seven students to pantomime the story as you tell it. You will need a traveler who gets wounded, two robbers, a priest, a Levite, a Samaritan helper, and an innkeeper. Talk with the actors about what they should do. Caution the robbers not to be rough.

> Jesus told a story about a man who was traveling from Jerusalem to Jericho (*walks around the room*) when he was attacked by robbers (*robbers attack walker*). They beat him, stole his money, and left him lying on the roadside (*he falls down and lies there*). When a priest came by that way and saw the injured man, he quickly walked on by (*walks quickly around fallen man*). A little later, a Levite came by and saw the half-dead man. He, too, passed by without stopping to help the man (*hurries by fallen man*). Then a Samaritan came by. He stopped to see if he could help the injured man (*stops and helps fallen man*). He bandaged his wounds, lifted him onto his own donkey, took him to an inn, and took care of him (*helps man to a chair*). When the Samaritan had to leave and the injured man was still not well, he gave the innkeeper some money and asked him to care for the man (*count out money to innkeeper*). He promised to pay him whatever else he owed him the next time he stopped by.
>
> Samaritans and Jews did not like each other, so it was surprising that the Samaritan was willing to help the injured man. Surely, the priest or Levite, religious leaders, were the ones who should have helped him. But they were concerned only about themselves. They either did not care or were unwilling to take time to help a needy person. The love that the Samaritan showed was the kind of love Jesus said we should show to our neighbors every day.

Discussion

On May 1, people traditionally give May baskets of spring flowers to show their love. Have you ever given anyone a May basket? Often the baskets are secretly left on a doorstep or doorknob so the person who receives it does not know who brought it. This is a fun way to cheer up neighbors and friends and to make new friends. What are some other ways you can show love for people in your neighborhood?

Bible Verse

"The entire law is summed up in a single command: 'Love your neighbor as yourself.'" (Galatians 5:14)

Why is loving others so important for a Christian? What has God done for us that should make us love other people?

Craft: May Day Doorknob Hanger

Materials

- patterns on page 117
- pipe cleaner
- scissors
- cardstock
- glue and tape
- crayons and markers

Craft: May Day Doorknob Hanger *(cont.)*

Directions

1. Copy the patterns on cardstock. Make two copies of the large one. Color and cut out. (*Option:* Use felt instead of cardstock.)
2. Bend a pipe cleaner. Place the pipe cleaner inside the flower and tape it in place. Glue the two flower shapes together, leaving the top open to form a pocket.
3. Glue the circle on the middle of the flower.
4. Fill the flower with candy, flowers, or a message and hang it on a doorknob as a reminder.

Love Your Neighbor As Yourself!

Love Your Neighbor As Yourself!

Finished Product

Bible Story: Peter Meets a Kind Woman (Acts 9:36-42)

Say the rap for students, then let students try saying it with you.

I heard of a woman who lived long ago;
Her name was Dorcas, and you should know
She was always doing good and being kind,
Helping the poor, letting her light shine.
One day Dorcas got sick and died.
Many people came to her house and cried.
They sent for Peter to come right away,
Maybe he could help; at least he could pray!
When Peter arrived everyone showed him
The clothes Dorcas made for all of them.
She'd been known for her kindness all over town,
For the helpfulness she'd spread all around.
Everyone left the room, but Peter stayed.
He got right down on his knees and prayed.
Then he looked at Dorcas and Peter said,
"Get up!" And she sat right up in bed!
He took her hand and helped her to her feet
And called back the people for her to greet.
Many people believed in Jesus then
Because they could see Dorcas was alive again!

Discussion

In what two ways was Dorcas a witness for Jesus? Dorcas was a good seamstress, so she used that talent to show kindness to people. What talent do you have that you can use to show kindness?

Bible Verse

"Be kind and compassionate to one another, forgiving each other, just as in Christ God forgave you." (Ephesians 4:32)

Why should we be kind to people? What does it mean to be compassionate?

Craft: "Bee" Kind Hang-up

Finished Product

Materials

- patterns below
- three 4" pipe cleaners
- magnetic strip
- crayons or markers
- cardstock
- tape and glue
- scissors

Directions

1. Copy the patterns on cardstock.
2. Color and cut them out.
3. Bend each pipe cleaner around a pencil to form a spring. Tape them in various places to the back of the beehive.
4. Glue or tape the bees to the ends of the pipe cleaners so they are "buzzing" around the hive.
5. Glue a magnetic strip to the back. Place on the refrigerator to help remind you to "Bee" kind.

"Bee"
Kind

"Be kind and compassionate to one another, forgiving each other, just as in Christ God forgave you."

(Ephesians 4:32)

Summer

Bible Story: Treasure Parables (Matthew 13:44-46; 6:19-21)

Choose two students to pantomime the two parables as you tell them. Talk with them ahead of time, going over the parables together so they can plan their actions.

Often Jesus told parables, stories, to teach people about God. One day He told two parables about the kingdom of God.

He said that once there was a man who found a treasure hidden in a field. He was so happy he did not know what to do! He jumped around and clapped his hands and hugged the treasure to himself. But then what? If he claimed the treasure for his own, the person who owned the field might say, "That's my treasure, not yours, because it was hidden in my field!" The man knew what he had to do. He quietly hid the treasure again so no one else would find it. He looked around to make sure no one had seen him; then he hurried home. He sold everything he owned to get enough money to buy that field. Of course, the owner didn't realize he was selling a treasure when he sold the man his field. But after that, the treasure rightfully belonged to the man who had found it. He paid a big price for it, but it was worth it!

Then Jesus told about a jewelry salesman who was looking for just the right pearls. One day he found a beauty! It was perfect—exactly what he wanted! He was so excited he could hardly stand it. He knew that pearl was worth a lot, so he went home and sold everything he owned. Then he used the money he got to buy that perfect pearl. He did not care that he'd had to sell his possessions for it. He treasured that pearl, and it was worth every penny he spent on it. He was happy to have it as his own.

God wants us to value His kingdom as much as the first man valued the treasure in the field and the second man valued the pearl. He wants to be most important in our lives.

Discussion

Someone once said, "God gives us things to use and people to love, but we usually get it backwards." What do you think that means? How can "things" turn our hearts away from the Lord? Why should God be most important in our lives?

Bible Verse

"For where your treasure is, there your heart will be also." (Matthew 6:21)

What do you care most about? Hopefully, it is not possessions because they're only temporary. God wants us to treasure eternal things like salvation.

Summer

Craft: Shoebox Treasure Chest

Finished Product

Materials

- patterns on pages 121 and 122
- markers or crayons
- glue sticks
- wrapping paper (blue or white)
- white paper
- shoebox
- scissors

Directions

1. Copy the patterns on white paper, color, and cut them out.
2. Cover the shoebox with blue or white wrapping paper. Wrap the lid separately.
3. Glue the sea art on the box.
4. Cut out the verse strips.
5. Put the verses in the treasure chest along with your special summer vacation treasures.

Verse Strips

"For where your treasure is,
there your heart will be also."
Matthew 6:21

"But store up for yourselves treasure in heaven,
where moth and rust do not destroy, and where
thieves do not break in and steal." Matthew 6:20

". . . salvation and wisdom and knowledge;
the fear of the Lord is the key to this treasure."
Isaiah 33:6

". . . never will I leave you;
never will I forsake you."
Hebrews 13:5

Craft: Shoebox Treasure Chest *(cont.)*

Sea Art Patterns

Summer

Bible Story: Nicodemus Visits Jesus (John 3:1-21)

Sing the song for students, then let them sing it with you.

(*Tune:* "B-I-N-G-O")

Jesus had a visitor; his name was Nicodemus.
Jesus said to him,
"Listen now, my friend,
You must be born again
To have eternal life."

Nicodemus didn't understand what He was saying.
"How can any man
Be born once again?
I don't understand.
Explain it, to me please."

Jesus said, "The second birth is from the Holy Spirit.
Life from Him that's new
He will give to you.
That's what you must do
To have eternal life."

If you give your life to Jesus, He'll change you completely.
Take your sin away,
Change your heart today,
So follow in His way
To have eternal life.

Bible Story: Nicodemus Visits Jesus (John 3:1-21) *(cont.)*

Discussion

To illustrate being born again, discuss the process of a caterpillar turning into a butterfly. Have you ever seen a cocoon? The caterpillar inside the cocoon seems dead for a long time. But what happens when the caterpillar emerges from the cocoon one day? *(It becomes a beautiful butterfly, a completely different creature.)* When we give our lives to Jesus, our old selves die, and He makes us new people. How can you tell when people have been born again? How are they different?

Bible Verse

". . . I tell you the truth, no one can see the kingdom of God unless he is born again." (John 3:3)

Encourage students to draw a sketch of a caterpillar turning into a butterfly and write this Bible verse on it.

Craft: Butterfly Mosaic

Materials

- pattern on page 125
- colored paper pieces
- cardstock
- glue sticks

Direction

1. Copy the pattern on cardstock.
2. Glue paper pieces on the butterfly. Cover it completely.

Variation: Cover the butterfly with colored craft foam shapes.

Finished Product

". . . no one can see the kingdom of God unless he is born again."
(John 3:3)

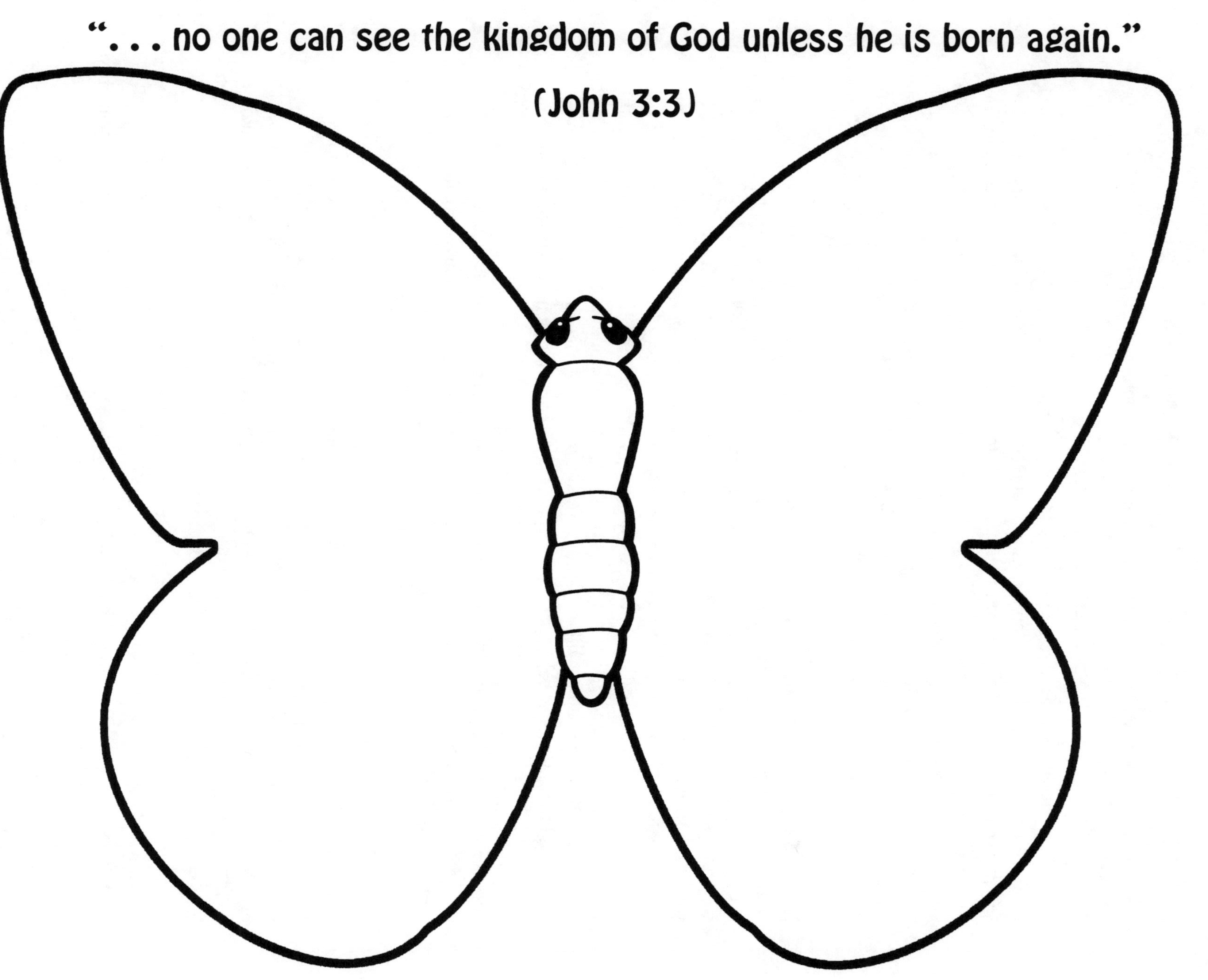
". . . no one can see the kingdom of God unless he is born again."
(John 3:3)

Summer

Bible Story: Jesus Grows Up (Luke 2:51-52; Bible customs)

As you tell about Jesus' childhood, encourage students to pantomime appropriate actions. Some suggestions are provided.

The Bible does not tell us much about how Jesus grew up. We know about His birth. We know wise men came to visit Him when He was a young child; then He and His family moved to Egypt to escape wicked King Herod. Some time later they came back and settled down in the town of Nazareth where Joseph worked as a carpenter. In Bible times, boys usually practiced whatever occupation their fathers practiced, carrying on the family business. Jesus probably worked in the shop with Joseph, learning how to saw and measure and hammer (*Pantomime these jobs*) to turn wood into useful objects such as tables and chairs. With none of the tools we have today to make the work easier, carpentry was hard work and Joseph probably never made much money.

Luke 2:52 tells us that Jesus grew, as all children do, in wisdom—mentally (*Point to head*) and stature—physically (*Raise hand from low to high*), and in favor with God—spiritually (*Put hand over heart*) and men—socially (*Shake hands with someone*). In addition to helping Joseph in the carpenter's shop, Jesus probably had chores to do in the house to help His mother: cleaning and filling lamps with oil, running errands, grinding grain, getting water from the town well, helping care for younger brothers and sisters (*Pantomime some of these jobs*). Of course, there was also time to play. Since Jesus didn't have expensive toys like children have today, he probably played with a homemade fabric ball or made His own slingshot. A popular game was digging a hole in the ground, then competing with a friend to see who could throw stones and get the most in the hole. And there were probably pet lambs to play with now and then. (*Pantomime some of these things.*)

At age six, Jewish boys started synagogue school; girls were not allowed. Jesus probably enjoyed school very much, hearing the teacher read God's Word aloud and explain it. He memorized Scripture and also learned to read and write in synagogue school (*Pretend to read a scroll and to write*). As he grew older, He probably learned math and geography and other subjects (*Count on fingers*).

One thing the Bible tells us clearly about Jesus' childhood is that He always obeyed His parents. Jesus never gave His parents a reason to have to punish Him because He never sinned. In every other way, He grew up much as you are growing up. He learned all He could about God, His Father, and about people. One day, He would give His life for people, so their sins could be forgiven. But in the meantime, Jesus worked and played and studied and did what His parents told Him, growing in favor with God and people.

Discussion

In what ways was Jesus' childhood like yours? In what ways was it different? How can you grow "in favor with God" as Jesus did?

Bible Verse

"And Jesus grew in wisdom and stature, and in favor with God and men." (Luke 2:52)

Jesus knew what God wanted Him to be when He grew up. What do you think God wants you to be?

Summer

Craft: Shape Book

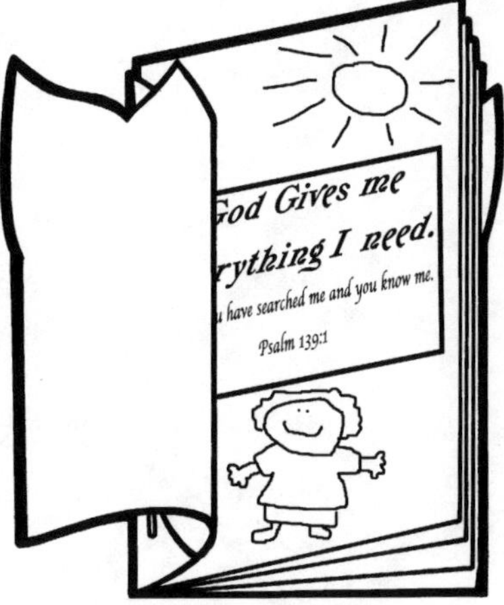

Finished Product

Materials

- patterns on pages 127 and 128
- crayons or markers
- stapler
- scissors
- cardstock
- white paper
- glue

Directions

1. Copy page 128 on cardstock.
2. Put two sheets of paper behind the front cover and fold them in half to form a booklet.
3. Staple the pages three times on the left side to hold the booklet together.
4. Cut the verses out and glue them in the booklet.
5. Draw pictures in the book and write about ways God helps you grow.

Verses

God knows all about me.

"O Lord, you have searched me and you know me." (Psalm 139:1)

God gives me everything I need.

". . . do not worry about your life, what you will eat or drink; or about your body, what you will wear." (Matthew 6:25a)

God gives parents to teach me.

"Listen, my son, to your father's instruction and do not forsake your mother's teaching." (Proverbs 1:8)

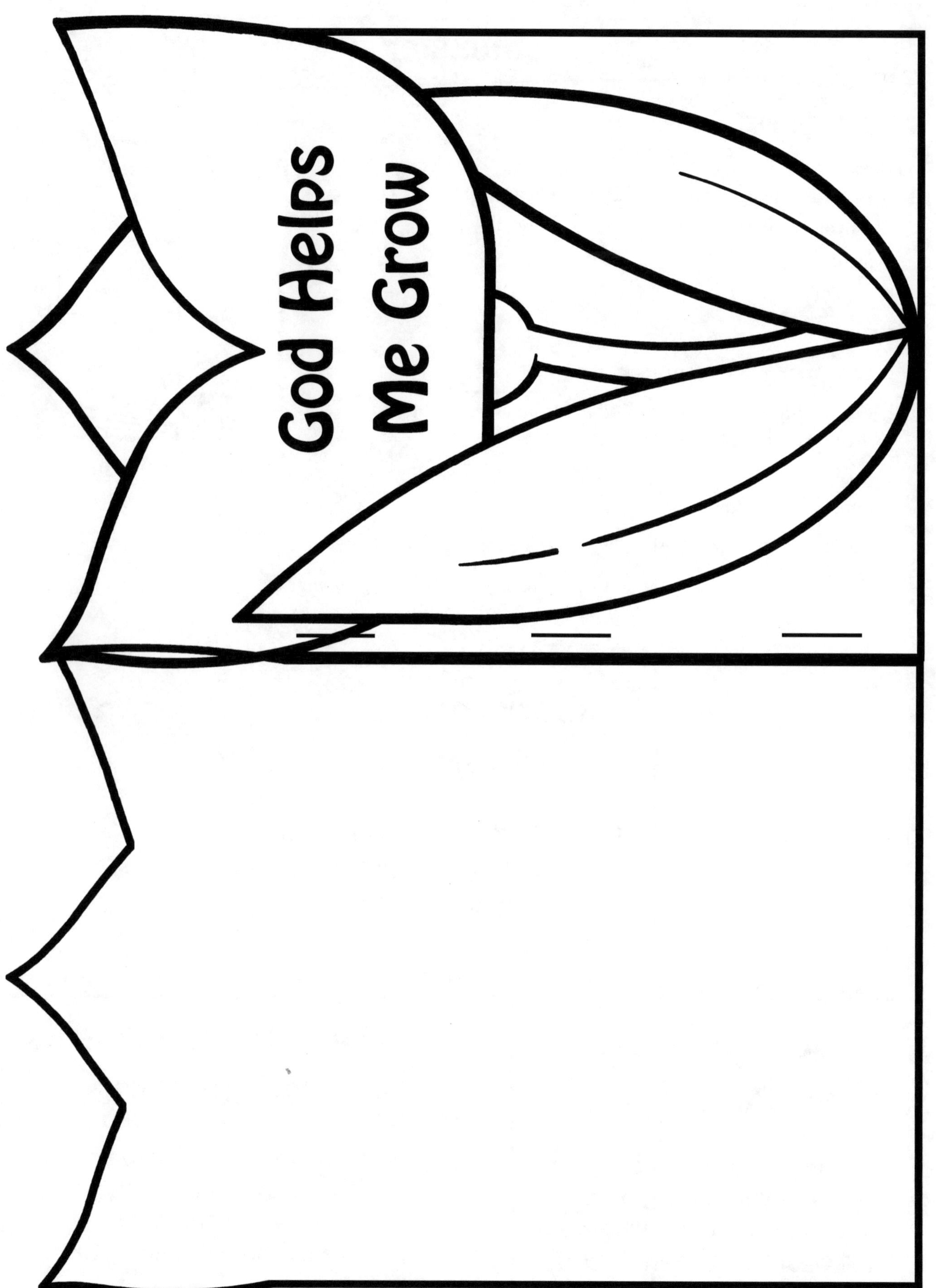
God Helps
Me Grow

Fall

Bible Story: Jesus Treats People Kindly (The Gospels)

As you discuss Jesus' experiences with people, ask questions to encourage students to think of how He treated them.

Throughout the first four books of the New Testament—Matthew, Mark, Luke, and John—we read about Jesus teaching and helping people. For example, when Peter's mother-in-law was sick, Jesus healed her. (Mark 1:29–34) That evening when people heard where Jesus was, the whole town came to the house bringing their sick friends and family members, hoping Jesus would heal them. Did Jesus tell them to go away because it was late and He was tired? *(No, he healed them and talked to them kindly.)*

When Jesus heard that His cousin John had been murdered, He got in a boat and went to a place where He could be alone. But when people heard where He was, more than five thousand of them came and found Him, bringing the sick with them again. Jesus wanted to be alone, but He was very patient with the people and healed the sick until late in the day. When evening came, instead of sending the hungry people all the way back to their homes to eat, He fed them. (Matthew 14:13–21) How did He feed them? *(With five loaves and two fish)* What was Jesus' attitude toward these people who had disturbed His peace? *(He had compassion on them.)*

One day some parents brought their young children to Jesus. (Matthew 19:13–15) What did his disciples do? *(They scolded the parents for bothering Jesus.)* What did Jesus do? *(Welcomed the children and blessed them.)*

Once Jesus met a Samaritan woman at a well. The woman was surprised when He spoke to her because men usually didn't speak to women in that culture, especially Samaritan ones! Most Jews and Samaritans disliked and avoided one another. But Jesus talked to her with kindness. He knew she was a sinful woman, but He did not accuse her or scold her. He talked with her about eternal life. (John 4) How did the woman respond to Jesus' words? *(She ran home and told everyone to come and see Jesus.)* Many of the people from her town believed in Jesus because of His kind treatment of that woman.

Even when His enemies were killing Him on a cross, Jesus forgave them. (Luke 23:34) Do you think Jesus ever mistreated anyone? Do you think He was ever unkind or impatient with people? (*Let students express their opinions.*) Jesus obeyed the Golden Rule, always treating people as He would like to be treated. That is what good manners is all about, putting other people first. As His disciples watched Jesus interact with people, they learned the importance of speaking and acting with kindness and humility instead of demanding their own way.

Discussion

When you're not sure how to respond to people, do you ever ask yourself the question "What would Jesus do?" How can that help you have good manners in every situation? September is Children's Good Manners Month. This is a great time to start working on having good manners and asking God to help you.

Bible Story: Jesus Treats People Kindly (The Gospels) *(cont.)*

Bible Verse

"Whatever happens, conduct yourselves in a manner worthy of the gospel of Christ." (Philippians 1:27a)

Why are good manners so important, especially for a Christian?

Craft: Good Manners Paper Plate Pocket

Materials

- patterns on pages 130 and 131
- scissors
- glue sticks
- crayons and markers
- two paper plates
- white paper
- stapler

Finished Product

Directions

1. Color and decorate the paper plates. Cut one of the paper plates in half.
2. Place one half on the lower half of the whole plate to form a pocket. Staple them together.
3. Cut out the verse below. Glue it on the paper plate pocket.
4. Copy the good manner cards on page 131 on white paper and keep them in the paper plate pocket.
5. Add other examples of good manners. Take them out and review them every day.

"Whatever happens, conduct yourselves in a manner worthy of the gospel of Christ." (Philippians 1:27)

Craft: Good Manners Paper Plate Pocket *(cont.)*

Good Manner Cards

Please

"Let your conversation be always full of grace. . . ."
Colossians 4:6

Thank You

"Give thanks in all circumstances."
1 Thessalonians 5:18a

Excuse Me

"Submit to one another out of reverence for Christ."
Ephesians 5:21

I'm Sorry

"Forgive as the Lord forgave you."
Colossians 3:13b

May I?

". . . clothe yourselves with compassion, kindness, humility, gentleness and patience."
Colossians 3:12

Fall

Bible Story: The Fruit of the Spirit (Matthew 7:15-20; Galatians 5:22-25)

Before you tell the story, cut a large apple shape from red paper. On one side print "BAD FRUIT;" on the other side print "GOOD FRUIT." Hold up the apple as directed in the story.

> One day Jesus took His disciples to a mountainside away from the crowds that always seemed to be following Him. He spent a long time teaching His twelve students some things they needed to know about loving and serving God. One of the important things Jesus talked about was fruit. He warned the disciples that there would always be false prophets around, wicked people who pretended to love God but really only wanted to lead people away from Him. "You will recognize them by their fruit," Jesus said. These people might say all the right things, such as "I love God and I want to serve Jesus." (*Hold up GOOD FRUIT side of apple.*) That sounds good, doesn't it? It might make the disciples decide that the people were believers in Jesus. They might listen to them and make friends with them. But Jesus said, you can't believe what everybody says! It is by people's actions and attitudes, their fruit, that we know what they are really like inside. (*Hold up BAD FRUIT side of apple.*) Some of those people who said all the right things didn't prove by their lives that they loved God. Jesus did not want His disciples to be fooled by dishonest prophets.
>
> What are some examples of bad actions, or fruit, that might show a person does not really love the Lord? (Students' ideas may include not going to church, using God's name disrespectfully, mistreating people, disobeying parents or teachers.) In the book of Galatians, Paul wrote a list of characteristics that show a person loves God. Can you name them? *(Love, joy, peace, patience, kindness, goodness, faithfulness, gentleness, and self-control)* These are called the fruit of the Spirit because they are characteristics the Holy Spirit puts in people who have given their lives to Jesus. The Holy Spirit does not live in unbelievers, so they do not demonstrate these characteristics as believers do. Paul said that believers, Christians, live by the Spirit. He guides us and helps us show our love for Jesus in all these ways.

Discussion

Talk about the fruit of the Spirit to make sure students understand all of them. Ask them to suggest ways we show these fruit in our everyday lives. (Examples: We show peace when we don't worry about things but trust God to do what is best for us. We show goodness when we refuse to go along with the crowd in doing wrong. We show self-control when we do not get angry.)

Bible Verse

"But the fruit of the Spirit is love, joy, peace, patience, kindness, goodness, faithfulness, gentleness and self-control." (Galatians 5:22–23a)

The Holy Spirit does not give us two or three of these characteristics; He gives them all to us!

Craft: Fall Door Hanger

Materials

- patterns on pages 133 and 134
- crayons or markers
- yarn or jute
- cardstock
- glue
- ribbon or fabric strips
- scissors
- tape

Fall

Craft: Fall Door Hanger *(cont.)*

Directions

1. Copy the patterns on cardstock. You will need nine apples. Color the apples and leaves.
2. Cut out the Fruit of the Spirit words. Glue one on each apple.
3. Cut five yarn or jute pieces 26–30" long. Tie a knot at the top of one end. Wrap ribbon or strips of fabric around the knot.
4. Tape the apples and leaves randomly on the yarn or jute. Hang them on the door.

Love

Patience

Joy

Goodness

Gentleness

Peace

Faithfulness

Kindness

Self-Control

Craft: Fall Door Hanger *(cont.)*

Fruit of the Spirit

Fruit of the Spirit
Love
Joy
Gentleness
Self-Control
Kindness

Finished Product

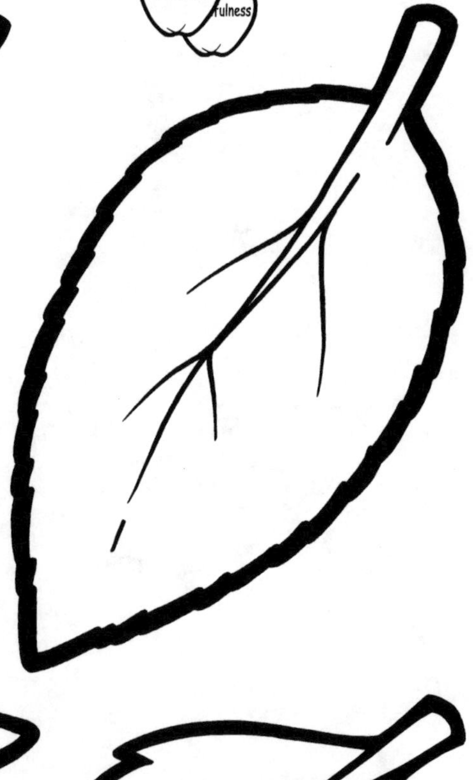

Fall

Bible Story: Stand up for the Lord (Daniel 3; Matthew 5:14-16)

Say the action rhyme with the actions; then have students say it with you.

King Nebuchadnezzar made a huge statue
(*Hold hand up high to indicate something very tall.*)
For everybody to bow down to.
(*Bow from the waist.*)
But Shadrach, Meshach, and Abednego
(*Count them off on your fingers.*)
Wouldn't bow down. They said, "No!
(*Stand stubbornly with hands on hips and shake head no.*)
We won't bow down to your image of gold.
(*Point as if at statue.*)
We'll only do what we are told—
(*Cross arms over chest.*)
By God!"
Nebuchadnezzar was so angry!
(*Shake fists and look mad.*)
"You'll burn for this!" he shouted with glee.
(*Point to someone and shake index finger.*)
The furnace was made hotter than before.
(*Wipe sweat off brow.*)
The three were tied and tossed through the door.
(*Pretend to throw the men into the furnace.*)
The king looked and then looked again!
(*Shade eyes with hand and look intently.*)
Inside the furnace he saw four men.
(*Put hands on cheeks and look shocked.*)
"Come out!" he said and out they came,
(*Gesture "come" with arm.*)
Completely untouched by smoke or flame.
(*Sweep hands over body to show you're okay.*)
God saved them and showed one and all
(*Sweep arm around to indicate many people.*)
When you stand up for Him, He won't let you fall!
(*Point to heaven; then give a thumbs up.*)

Bible Story: Stand up for the Lord (Daniel 3; Matthew 5:14-16) *(cont.)*

Discussion

Who was the fourth man the king saw in the furnace? Why did God protect Shadrach, Meshach, and Abednego? Do you think it was hard for them to stand up for God against the king? Why? Why is it sometimes hard for you to show that you love Jesus?

Bible Verse

". . . let your light shine before men, that they may see your good deeds and praise your Father in heaven." (Matthew 5:16)

Both your words and actions can show people that you love Jesus. Something as simple as book covers with Bible verses and Christian art on them can be a silent witness of your faith in Him. What are some other ways in which you can share your faith?

Craft: Book Covers

Materials

- patterns on page 137
- white paper
- plain-colored wrapping paper
- glue
- scissors
- colored markers

Directions

1. Copy the patterns on white paper. Color and cut them out.
2. Wrap your books with plain-colored wrapping paper.
3. Choose the art with which you want to decorate each cover. Glue the art in place. Add your own designs and words.

Finished Product

Craft: Book Covers *(cont.)*

". . . let your light shine before men, that they may see your good deeds and praise your Father in heaven." (Matthew 5:16)

I'm a King's Kid!

"Yet to all who receive him (Jesus) . . . he gave the right to become children of God." (John 1:12)

Temporary Student Headed for Heaven!

"For God so loved the world that he gave his one and only Son, that whoever believes in him shall not perish but have eternal life." (John 3:16)

Winter

Bible Story: God Cares About Animals (Matthew 10:29-31; Psalm 104)

As you tell the story, ask questions for students to answer. Most of the questions are opinion questions, so there are no right or wrong answers.

One day Jesus was assuring His disciples that God loved them and would take care of them. As an example, He began talking about sparrows. There were probably sparrows hopping along the ground near them or flying in the sky. Jesus pointed out that the sparrow was the most common bird around. There were many thousands of them, so many that most people didn't even notice them. But God noticed. Jesus said that God was aware of every time a little sparrow fell to the ground. Which do you think God loves more—sparrows or people? Why?

Jesus knew God's Word and had memorized Scripture. He probably had read Psalm 104 many, many times. The Psalm describes the amazing world God created and reminds us that God cares for each part of His creation. He is the One who makes springs flow between mountains, providing water for wild animals to drink, and trees nearby where birds can build their nests. He makes grass grow for cattle and deer. What other animals eat grass? He created tall mountains where wild goats climb and small animals hide. What small animals hide in mountain caves and holes? God made darkness, a time when lions prowl around searching for food. What other animals search for food at night? God made the sea and filled it with so many fish and sea creatures, no one could ever count them all. How do all these animals survive? The psalm writer wrote, "These all look to you to give them their food at the proper time. When you give it to them, they gather it up; when you open your hand, they are satisfied with good things." (Psalm 104:27–28)

God cares about each one of His creatures, no matter how tiny. And He cares even more about us.

Discussion

In what ways does God care for animals throughout the year? What special abilities did He give some animals to help them survive cold weather? What are some other ways God shows that He cares about animals as well as people?

Bible Verse

"How many are your works, O Lord! In wisdom you made them all; the earth is full of your creatures." (Psalm 104:24)

What is your favorite animal? Why? Let's thank God for them.

Winter

Craft: Animals-in-Winter Picture

Materials

- patterns on pages 139 and 140
- crayons or markers
- glue or tape
- cardstock
- scissors

Directions

1. Copy patterns on cardstock.
2. Color and cut out patterns of animals and place in the scene (page 140).

Animal Patterns

"How many are your
works, O Lord! In
wisdom you made
them all; the earth is
full of your creatures."
(Psalm 104:24)

Winter

Bible Story: Jesus and Joy (John 15:9-14; 16:33)

Seat all students around a table or in a circle of chairs with you at the front. Hand out small crackers and cups of juice and let them pretend they are the disciples eating a meal with Jesus. (*Note:* Check for any food allergies.)

The night before Jesus was arrested, He ate the Passover meal with His disciples. He knew He didn't have much longer with them, and He had some important things to tell them. He knew they would be upset and confused by His death. He had told them He was going to die, but they didn't understand. What did He want them to remember? Amazingly, Jesus talked to His friends about joy! Even though He was going to die soon, He wanted them to be joyful. He said, "As the Father has loved me, so I have loved you. If you obey my commands, you will remain in my love." Then Jesus told them that if they loved Him, they would have great joy. He wanted them to love each other as much as He loved them. He called them His friends and encouraged them by telling them they would face trouble in the world, but He had overcome the world.

Knowing that Jesus loved them would help the disciples get through the hard times that were coming soon. They would learn that no matter what was happening around them, they could have joy in their hearts because of His love.

Of course, Jesus' promise of love wasn't just for His disciples back then; it was for us, too. Knowing that Jesus loves us gives us joy that nothing else can bring. Being a Christian is not just about obeying God and doing the right thing. It is about cheerfully serving Him with a joyful heart.

Discussion

There's a chorus that says, "The joy of the Lord is my strength." What do you think that means? When do you find it hard to smile? How can you remember to show the joy of the Lord during those times? A happy snowman in the winter reminds us that God wants us to be joyful. If the snowman can smile with cold feet, so can we even when things are not exactly the way we want them!

Bible Verse

"A cheerful heart is good medicine." (Proverbs 17:22a)

How can a cheerful heart from you bring joy to someone else's heart? Why should Christians be even more cheerful than other people?

Craft: Snowman Magnet

Materials

- patterns on page 142
- white cardstock
- glue
- magnet
- markers
- scissors

Craft: Snowman Magnet *(cont.)*

Directions

1. Copy the patterns below on cardstock and cut them out.
2. Glue the hat on the snowman head.
3. Use markers to draw a face. Use an orange marker to draw a nose.
4. Glue a magnet on the back of the snowman and put it on the refrigerator to remind you to be cheerful.

Variation: Use craft foam instead of cardstock paper.

Finished Product

Snowman Head Pattern

Hat Pattern

"A cheerful heart

is good medicine."

(Proverbs 17:22a)

Winter

Bible Story: Special to God (Psalm 139)

Choose 10 students to stand in front. As you talk about each of the ways we are special to God, lay your hand on a student's head or shoulder. The student may sit down when you go to the next student to explain another way we are special to God. Remember to include the rest of the class each time, so every student understands that he or she is special to God.

> Did you know that you are special to God? Psalm 139 was written by David to remind us how we are special to Him.
>
> 1. You are special to God because He knows everything about you, things that no one else knows. And He still loves you. That's how you're special to God.
> 2. You are special to God because He sees everything you do. He sees when you sit or stand or walk or run, go to sleep or wake up. That's how you're special to God.
> 3. You are special to God because He knows all the thoughts you're thinking. He's a mind reader! You can't hide your thoughts from Him. That's how you're special to God.
> 4. You are special to God because He knows what you're going to say before you say it. That's how you're special to God.
> 5. You are special to God because He's with you everywhere; you can't get away from Him. No matter where you go, God is there too. That's how you're special to God.
> 6. You are special to God because He formed you inside your mother. He's the One who made you exactly the way you are because that's the way He wanted you to be. That's how you're special to God.
> 7. You are special to God because He knew all about you before you were even conceived. He already planned what color of hair you would have, what your personality would be like, and what talents He would give you. That's how you're special to God.
> 8. You are special to God because He is thinking about you all the time. He's helping you even when you don't know it and taking care of you. That's how you're special to God.
> 9. You are special to God because He watches over you day and night, protecting and caring for you. That's how you're special to God.
> 10. You are special to God because He knows your heart as no one else can. He knows when you say you love Him if you really mean it. He understands your concerns and disappointments and weaknesses. That's how you are special to God.

Discussion

How does being special to God make you feel? There is one big way, the biggest, God showed how special you are to Him that David didn't mention. What is it? *(He sent Jesus to die for our sins.)*

Bible Verse

"I praise you because I am fearfully and wonderfully made." (Psalm 139:14a)

What do you think is wonderful about the way God made you?

Winter

Craft: "You Are Special" Snowflakes

Materials

- pattern below
- white cardstock
- Christmas ornament wire hanger
- silver glitter
- glue
- scissors

Finished Product

Directions

1. Copy the pattern on white cardstock and cut it out.
2. Use the glue to make a snowflake design on the pattern.
3. Sprinkle with glitter. Shake off excess glitter and let dry.
4. Poke a hole in the top of the snowflake and use a Christmas ornament wire hanger to hang it.

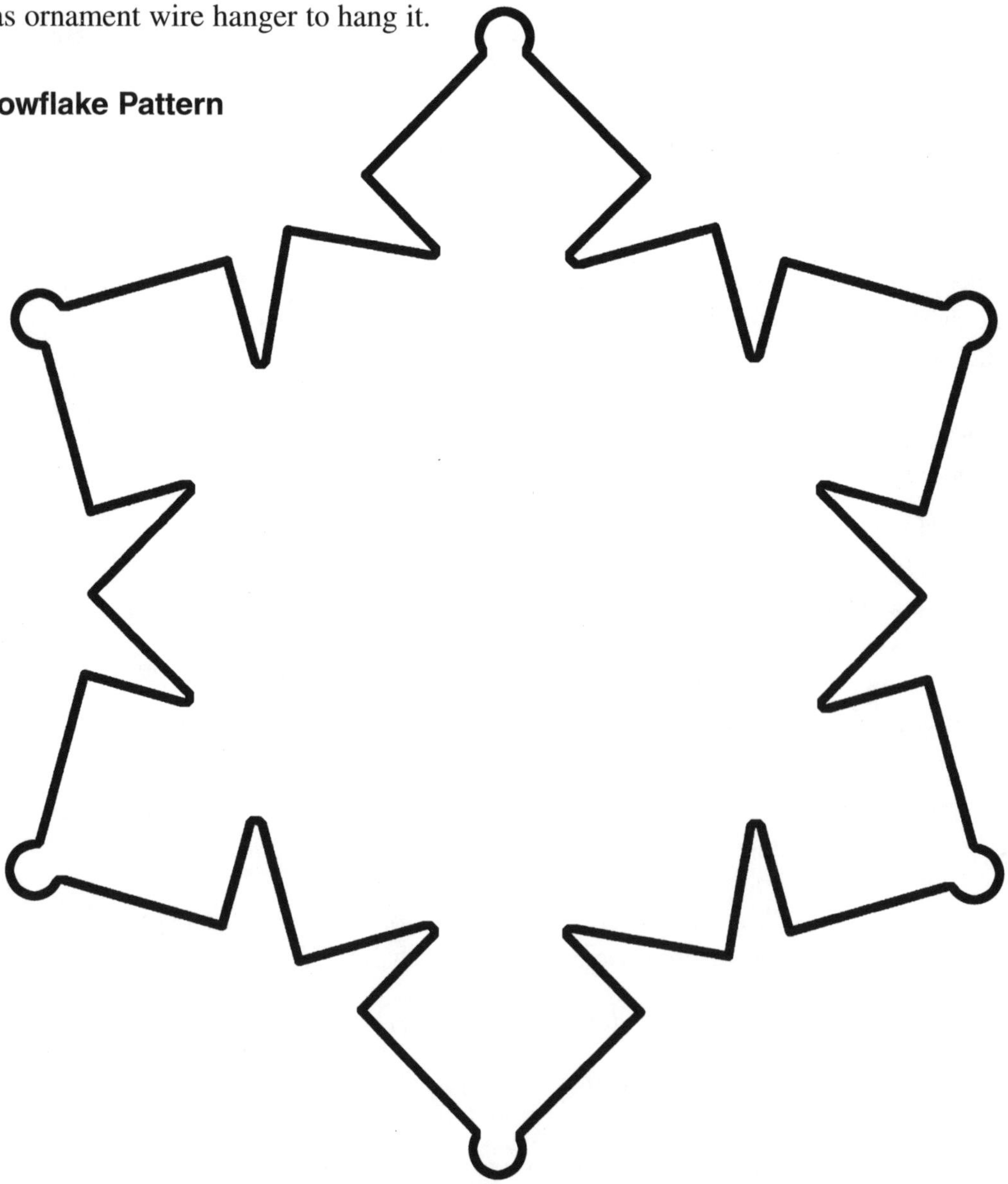

Snowflake Pattern